MATURE CHRISTIANS ARE BORING PEOPLE...

AND OTHER MYTHS ABOUT MATURITY IN CHRIST

By RON LUCE

ALBURY PUBLISHING
Tulsa, Oklahoma

Mature Christians Are Boring...
And Other Myths About Maturity
ISBN 1-57778-037-X
Copyright © 1997 by Ron Luce
P.O. Box 2000
Garden Valley, TX 75771

Published by ALBURY PUBLISHING
P.O. Box 470406
Tulsa, OK 74147-0406

Cover design and production by:
Paragon Communications Group, Inc.
Tulsa, Oklahoma

CONTENTS

DEDICATION

This book is dedicated to all the teenagers who are passionately pursuing God's presence in their lives and who have committed their lives to changing the world.

ACKNOWLEDGMENTS

A big thank you to my wife Katie, who together with me has helped to formulate the principles you are about to read. I also want to express my appreciation to Joni Jones who edited this book, and the young ladies: Alece Ronzino, Kimberly Houle, Dawn Stauffer, Beth McNinch, Charlene Garrett, and Sarah Baltzley who worked many hours typing and researching this book. I also want to express appreciation to my executive assistant Michelle Franzen for all she has put up with in the process of putting this book together. Together, all of our efforts will help equip teens to change the world.

INTRODUCTION

Something is about to happen. God is up to something with young people all over North America and around the world. There is a stir in the air. There is a restlessness in the hearts of average church-going teens wanting something deeper. There is an emptiness in the hearts of non-Christian young people wanting to find something real. There is a stir in the hearts of youth leaders wanting something to explode in this generation of young people. There is a cry towards heaven from parents and grandparents all around this world wanting God to do something to intervene in the hearts and lives of this young generation.

Tens of thousands of teenagers are on their knees every morning crying out to God in their Quiet Times. Millions of them are meeting at flagpoles to pray every year. There is a seriousness in the eyes of those who used to be lukewarm believers. Something is about to happen in the schools where the rebellious once took charge. Where rebellion once ruled, righteousness will invade. Where peer pressure to live an ungodly life used to rule, peer pressure to live a godly, righteous, and holy life will prevail. Where immorality and promiscuity used to be the norm, purity, chastity, and holiness will become normal.

People are going to get saved, set free, turned on. Holy fervor and passion for God will explode in the hearts of this generation. Once you were persecuted and thought weird for praying over your meals in the cafeteria. In days to come, people in schools all across this land will think it strange if you do not pray over your food. It used to be an exception to the rule when a ball player would kneel and pray before a football game. Soon it will be thought strange if the whole team doesn't kneel and fervently cry out to God before every ball game. It's time to think and dream big because God has a BIG heart for an entire generation. It's time for us to dare to imagine and dream of His coming in and sweeping over this generation with His power affecting every realm of life. Movies geared toward teen rebellion and promiscuity will be unprofitable because teens won't go see that garbage. The music industry, built on teen rebellion and drugs, will find itself losing billions of dollars because the hearts of the young people are turned toward God.

The question is this: Are you ready for all this? Are you ready for what God is about to do in your generation? Are you ready to be part of the answer? As God gets ready to unveil Himself in a massive way, He's looking for young people who will step up to the plate and be leaders. Young people who will step up and help lead a revival. Young people who are determined to be strong and mature in their Christian life. Young people whose roots are deep into the Word of God. Young people who know more than John 3:16 and who are ready to disciple their generation as God sweeps them off their feet. God is looking for young people who will be WorldChangers, who will say it is time to go beyond surface Christianity and go on and grow in the deep things of God. Young people who want to be a significant part of history by preparing themselves to lead their generation in revival.

Think of the young people who are determined to develop character and the lifestyle of a mature Christian—that is what this book is all about. It's a devotional designed for you to use every day in your Quiet Time. This book has something for you to do every day to help you grow up into that man or woman God is desiring you to be. You're going to learn a lot about being a mature Christian. You'll see that you don't have to be old in years to be a mature Christian.

It would be great for you to get an accountability partner to go through this book with, or go through it with your entire youth group. Push each other to go after God and become the strong men and women that God is wanting you to be.

COMMITMENT FORM

I commit to go through all 13 weeks of the devotional.

Signature _____

Youth Pastor's Signature _____

WEEK ONE

....

WHAT IS MATURITY ANYWAY?

DAY ONE: YOU DON'T BECOME BORING WITH MATURITY.

The Bible has a lot to say about maturing in Christ. It talks a lot about our growing up in the Lord. The problem, though, is the word "maturity." It is a very boring word. The very word implies that you become stuffy, petrified, "a stick in the mud." It implies that becoming mature is when you quit having fun and decide to live a dull life. With all this in mind, teenagers especially shy away from the whole idea of maturing or growing up. But nothing could be further from the truth when it comes to growing up in Christ.

I first got on fire for the Lord when I was sixteen years old. I talked a hundred miles a minute about how God had changed my life, how thrilled I was to be saved, how cool it was to be a Christian, and how excited I was to really know Jesus. The impression I got from people was, "Don't worry. After a while, you will calm down." It was almost as if they were saying that when you get "mature in Jesus" you won't be so excited. Well, if that is maturity, I don't want it. But as you will soon see, that is not what maturity in Christ is. In fact, as you grow in the Lord and get closer to him, you ought to be more excited. When you learn more about God, how could it possibly make you more calm? It should make you more thrilled to be saved and to be close to Him.

➡ THE FIRST MYTH ABOUT MATURITY: ⬅

IF YOU BECOME MATURE, YOU WILL BE A BORING PERSON AND A BORING CHRISTIAN.

There are many examples in the Scriptures that prove this myth wrong. Look at Moses, for example. The older he got, the more incredible his adventures with God became: going to Mount Sinai, seeing the burning bush, leading 3 million people through the Red Sea.

Daniel 11:32 says, ...*But the people that do know their God shall be strong, and do exploits.*

Note that it says that those who "know" their God shall be strong and do great exploits. Maturity has to do with really knowing God. This is not a superficial knowing about God. It is knowing Him heart and soul, knowing His mind, how He thinks, and the way He does things. The closer you get to God, the more mature you get and the more exploits you will do. In other words, the more mature you get, the more wild things God will trust you with to impact this world. Do you want to do wild things? Do you want to live on the cutting edge? Do you want to be on the strategic front of what God is doing to absolutely change this world? Then you have to know Him, I mean really know Him. You have to grow, get mature, get strong. You have to dive into the deep things of God.

The dictionary says that to be mature is to be fully grown, fully developed. It means to be highly developed, perfected, and worked out, having reached maximum development, and being complete. The Greek definition of maturity refers to growth, mental and moral character, completeness. So many Christians walk around not fully grown. That is, they remain babies in Christ their whole lives, only half there. They are not complete Christians; they are surfacey Christians.

Spend the rest of your prayer time this morning asking God about different areas that He wants you to grow so you can become a mature man or woman of God. List some of these areas here:

_____

_____

_____

DAY TWO: MATURITY IN CHRIST IS MEASURED BY YOUR OBEDIENCE TO THE WORD OF GOD.

➡ THE SECOND MYTH ABOUT MATURITY: ⬅

THE SECOND MYTH ABOUT MATURITY: THE LONGER YOU GO TO CHURCH, THE MORE MATURE IN CHRIST YOU BECOME.

People think that just going to church every week makes them strong in the Lord. Don't get me wrong, going to church can help you grow. But just because you go to church does not mean that you are mature. There are many people who have been going to church all their life, and some of them have never even made the decision to give their life to Jesus in a personal way. Others who have gone to church their whole life and made a decision when they were a child, but they've never really done anything to grow in the Lord. Yet they think that because they have been in church all their life they are strong Christians or mature believers.

Maturity in Christ is not measured by years. Maturity in Christ is measured by your obedience to the Word of God. The more obedient you are, the more mature you are. The more you live what the Bible says, the more you show that you are a mature believer, no matter how old you are. I have seen thirteen-, fourteen-, fifteen-year-old teenagers who were extremely mature in Christ. They are young physically, but they are towers of strength spiritually.

Hebrews 5:12: *In fact, though by this time you ought to be teachers, you need someone to teach you the elementary truths of God's Word all over again. You need milk, not solid food!*

Write out in your own words what you think this means:

_____

_____

_____

_____

Think about the words "by this time." The writer of Hebrews is saying "Listen! You guys have been going to church for a long time. You have been hanging around other believers for a long time. You have had enough time. You should have grown up by now. Just because you have been hanging around does not mean that you have grown up. You are still acting like babies."

This is the state of so much of the church. We have so many gray-haired babies in churches all over the world. They are old physically, so they think they are spiritually mature; but this is not necessarily the case. Now, time is part of growing up as a Christian. You cannot think that you can become mature overnight—that you just get zapped, and you are Robo-Christian. It is time spent regularly applying the Word of God to your life that helps you to grow up, not just time by itself. In other words, you have to be using your time wisely as a Christian—time in church and time between Sundays— so that you are maximizing your opportunity for growth.

If you feel that you've been around church a lot (or even your whole life) and haven't really grown much, it's not too late. Take advantage of the time you have now to make sure that all of your time counts toward growing in the Lord. Ask the Lord how you can make the best use of your time to make sure you are not just growing physically, but also spiritually.

DAY THREE: GROWTH IN THE LORD IS LIKE MUSCLE DEVELOPMENT.

THE THIRD MYTH ABOUT MATURITY:

ONCE YOU GROW IN A CERTAIN AREA, YOU CAN NEVER LOSE THAT GROWTH OR MATURITY.

Growing in the Lord is different from growing physically. Once you reach the age of fifteen, you can't go back to the age of fourteen physically. Once you reach the age of eighteen, you can't go back to the age of seventeen physically, obviously. We start thinking that once we have learned a certain thing about the Lord, or grown in a certain area, we will never be weak in that area again.

Many people go to a revival, a convention, or a camp where God does something in their life. The tendency is to think, "Now I know that I will never fall or be weak in that area again." Unfortunately, that is simply not true. Growth in the Lord is like muscle development. You have to continue to exercise that muscle in order for it to stay strong. If you do not, it will get flabby and weak. Many of you who work out with weights know that if you don't continue to work out, you can't keep pumping the same amount of iron.

Many Christians are like an elderly person with a disease whose mind don't work very well. You may have seen people with a sickness that causes them to revert to thinking or acting as if they were children or infants. That's what a lot of Christians look like. They're "mature," so they think, because they have been in church their whole life. But, they still drool like a baby, act like a baby, and prove by their very lives that they're very immature.

2 John 8: *Watch out that you do not lose what you have worked for.*

Write out what you think that means: _____

_____

_____

_____

Look at this verse carefully. Do not lose what you have worked for. There are some things in Christ that we have to work for if we want them. Now, we know that salvation is a free gift of God (Romans 6:23). There is nothing that we can do to earn it with our own works (Titus 3:5). We give our whole life to Jesus, and He gives us a brand new heart. He changes our life. We can't earn any of this. There is nothing we can do to be good enough for God.

Once we have received the free gift of salvation and the new heart and changed life, there are some things that we need to earn and work for if we want them. One of the things that we work for is maturity in Christ. You don't get maturity by praying for it. You do not get maturity by wanting it or hoping for it. You get maturity in Christ by working for it. You get maturity by working on different areas of your life that God wants you to grow in. That is what this book is about—learning how to work "with God" using His Word on different areas of your life to help you to grow.

You do not get mature by going to another revival and asking God to "zap" you when somebody prays for you. When you are thirteen, you cannot pray, "Oh, God please make me eighteen years old tomorrow." No matter how much you pray that, you still have to live it. You cannot say, "Oh, God, even though I can only lift 100 pounds, please make me lift 250 pounds tomorrow." No, if you want that kind of maturity in your muscles, you're going to have to work for it. In the same way, if you want maturity in Christ, you need to decide right now that you are going to be the kind of person who works for it. You have to say, "I don't care how hard it is, or how long it takes, I refuse to be a baby Christian my whole life. I refuse to be a baby Christian even this next year of my life. It is time to grow up."

I encourage you to make that decision as you dive into some prayer time and tell the Lord that you are serious about paying the price. Whatever it takes, no matter how hard you have to work to grow up as a Christian, you must be willing to do it.

DAY FOUR: YOU NEED TO GROW UP IN YOUR SALVATION.

1 Peter 2:2: *Like newborn babies, crave pure spiritual milk, so that by it you may grow up in your salvation....*

Peter is encouraging us to grow up in our salvation. Just because you prayed the prayer does not mean that you have grown up. Just because you were born into the world as a person obviously doesn't mean that you are a full-grown adult. In the same way, just because you were born again into the Kingdom does not mean that you're a full-grown Christian. You have to grow up in your salvation. You have to get stronger in your salvation. You have to get mature in your salvation.

I want you to take a few minutes and just meditate on this verse. When I say meditate, I mean I want you to read it over and over and over and over again. Think about what it means. Take as much time as you need to memorize it.

Write out some things that you think you can do this week to grow up in your salvation:

_____

_____

_____

_____

Take this Scripture with you all day today. Chew on it all day with the commitment, *"Lord, I am going to grow up in my salvation. The Bible says to do it, and I am going to do it. I have grown a little bit, but I am not grown up yet."*

DAY FIVE: GOD WANTS US TO GROW UP IN ALL THINGS.

Ephesians 4:15: *Instead speaking the truth in love, we will in all things grow up into him who is the head, that is, Christ.*

Some people's idea of growth in their Christian life is knowing a lot more worship songs than other people. They may really shout, "Praise the Lord." Maybe they are genuinely good worshippers. Others have Quiet Times every day. All these things are great, but there are many things to grow up in. Here the Bible exhorts us to grow up in all things. So, for example, maybe you have really grown up in the practice of having a Quiet Time and being consistent to do it every day. But maybe it has become a ritual to you, and you really aren't getting anything out of it. Or maybe you are a great worshipper and you really worship your heart out at church, but you have not really learned to worship at home or in your Quiet Time. Or maybe you are a great worshipper, but you don't act in love towards other people at school all day long. Or maybe you are not very quick to forgive people. Or you murmur under your breath at your parents when they want you to do something that you do not want to do. So, in one part of your life you feel really strong, and you think that you are strong a Christian in every part. Yet, you have this glaring outage in other parts of your life that you are still not very strong in.

Paul wrote to the Ephesians, *You know what, there are a lot of areas God wants us to grow in.* There are a lot of areas where the world has trained us to live and act like heathens, to live and act like the world shows us in music, movies, and television. God wants to affect all those areas of our life. He wants to influence us in the way that we think, the way we feel, the way we respond to people and situations, and in our personal habits that nobody knows anything about. He wants us to grow up in all things—not most things, not some things, but all things. Now, you can't grow up in all things at once, but He still wants us to grow up in all things. It's time for us to start documenting areas we know we are not grown in so we can begin to ask the Lord, *"God, how do You want me to grow in these areas?"*

Take a moment and list the areas right now that you know you need to grow in—areas that if you were completely honest, you would know that you are really underdeveloped in:

_____

_____

_____

_____

_____

_____

_____

_____

_____

_____

_____

_____

_____

Now begin to pray, *"Lord, there are so many ways that I can grow in these areas so that I can grow in all things. Lord, I will be obedient and start working on these areas now."*

DAY SIX: THE MORE OF THE BIBLE YOU HEAR, THE MORE YOUR FAITH WILL GROW.

2 Corinthians 10:15: *Our hope is that, as your faith continues to grow, our area of activity among you will greatly expand.*

One area that God wants us to grow in is our faith. You might wonder, "How does my faith grow? Does it just happen by accident? Will it grow the more Quiet Times that I have, or the more I go to church? Will my faith automatically grow?" Not so. Does faith grow because I got in the car this morning and said *"Okay, I believe, I believe, I believe, I've got more and more faith"*? No, faith is just like that muscle we talked about earlier. You have to learn how to use your faith. The more you use it, the stronger it gets.

The Bible also says in Romans that faith comes by hearing the Word of God (Romans 10:17). In other words, the more of the Bible you hear, the more your faith will grow. The more you hear, the more you will actually believe what you are reading because the truth of that Scripture will explode in your heart.

For example, read James 1:17 which says, *Every good and perfect gift is from above, coming down from the Father of the heavenly lights.* You know in your mind this Scripture is true, but all your life you have heard things like, *"God did this to me,"* or *"This bad thing happened."* You have heard people get mad at God for a husband or wife leaving them. You know in your mind that God gives good things, but you have been bombarded with hearing these bad things people thought God had brought their way. So it's hard for you to be fully convinced that God really is a good God. In your mind you think, *"Yeah, He is a good God, but..."* That big BUT keeps your faith from growing in this area of believing that God is a good God.

Instead, take that Scripture and start chewing on it. *"I know that every good and perfect gift comes down from the Father of lights."* Say it over and over. *"That is the kind of God my God is. He gives good gifts. He gives perfect gifts. I don't care what other people say. I don't care what I have always heard. I know that the Bible says this is the kind of God He is."* Suddenly your faith begins to grow. When somebody starts to point a finger at God to shaft Him, you say, *"Wait a minute…"* You rise up on the inside because that part of your faith is strong and you know what the Bible says about who God is and the kind of gifts He gives.

Maybe there is another area where your faith is weak. Maybe it's hard for you to believe that God really forgave you. You know in your mind that He did because the Bible says that if you ask then He will forgive you (1 John 1:9). But it's so hard for you to forgive yourself and other people. You know in your mind that He forgave you, but it's hard to feel the freedom that a forgiven person really feels. So take a forgiveness Scripture and start cramming it in your brain. You realize that God has cast your sins as far as the east is from the west (Psalm 103:12)—chew on that again and again. All of the sudden you will realize that it's really true, not because you have pumped yourself up, but because your faith has grown as you have chewed on it and meditated on it.

Take a moment and list a few areas you have had weak faith in. In other words, it has been hard for you to believe that God is really a _____ kind of God.

_____

_____

_____

Now, I want you to dive into your Bible or ask your youth Pastor, your Pastor, or your parents for a Scripture that talks about those areas. Write those Scriptures out here:

_____

_____

_____

_____

_____

Now, take these Scriptures and begin to cram them down your throat and pray, *"Lord, I want my faith to grow in this area. And I know that it will grow as I continue to hear Your Word, God, even as it comes out of my mouth as I recite this Scripture over and over."*

DAY SEVEN: WHAT IS MATURITY ANYWAY?

Take some time this morning to review your memory verses for this week. Take a few minutes and review all of the things that you have written down this week, areas you want to grow in and areas you have been praying about. After you have reviewed them all, answer these questions:

What is your definition of maturity in Christ?

_____

_____

_____

_____

_____

Is it possible to lose your maturity in Christ once you have gained it? Why or why not?

_____

_____

_____

_____

_____

How do you keep your maturity in Christ?

_____

_____

_____

_____

_____

After you have reviewed this week's Quiet Times, accept my challenge to make a solemn commitment to God to do whatever it takes to mature. Be on a quest with your life. Begin to grow up right now as a Christian. Determine to grow in the Lord, whether people around you are doing it or not. Grow up and be mature. Get strong and know your God so that you can do great exploits for Him the rest of your life. Make that decision now before you go on to week two.

ACTION POINTS

What am I going to do in response to what I learned this week?

_____

_____

_____

_____

_____

_____

_____

_____

_____

_____

_____

_____

_____

_____

_____

_____

....

SIGNS OF IMMATURITY

DAY ONE: BEING HYPED IS NOT THE SAME AS BEING MATURE.

Roller-Coaster Christianity. We have all seen it happen either to us or to our friends. One minute we're totally hyped on God, and the next minute we're totally depressed. One minute we're feeling like we are going to change the whole world, the next minute we are wondering if we're even saved. Typical Roller-Coaster Christianity.

This is what seems to be normal for teens in their relationship with the Lord. Go to a camp, go to a concert, get totally psyched for God, and then, BOOM, reality hits the next day or the next week and they wonder if what happened was even real or not. This is a typical sign of immaturity in Jesus. Sometimes it is misinterpreted. People think that because they're hyped for God they must be strong. And then they get totally wacked out when they make a mistake. They think, *"Wow, I was really strong and I blew it. So even when I am strong, I'll blow it.*

Being hyped is not the same as being mature. We mentioned last week that just because you are mature doesn't mean that you don't have any excitement or fervor for God, but there's a maturity in our fervor and in our enthusiasm for God that goes beyond just the "hype" session that takes you to the top of a roller coaster. God is not interested in giving us a cheerleading session to "hype" us up for the day. He is interested in building us up, not hyping us up. He wants the joy and the thrill that we have in our Christian life not to come from emotionalism or from adrenaline. Genuine joy that comes from the throne of God is in knowing that we are saved and that Jesus lives inside of us.

Look up Ephesians 4:14 and write it out here.

_____

_____

_____

_____

_____

Here is a Scripture that talks about no longer being infants tossed about. What it is saying is that infants, or people who are young in their faith, are tossed about. They get blown by this temptation, blown by that doctrine, blown by this Christian band, blown again by that preacher. They're blown around so much that they don't know where they're going or what they're doing. They are back and forth, up and down, sometimes hot, sometimes not.

You cannot measure people's maturity in Christ by whether or not they're hyped. The measurement is how stable they are. Is their fervor for God continuing, or is it just something they're in the mood for right now?

If you have been on a roller coaster ride for God, it is time to stop. Get off the roller coaster and say, *"God, I want You to fill me with real joy."* Pray like David prayed in Psalm 51, *Restore to me the joy of your Salvation.* In other words, "Let me get really psyched about what has really happened in me, and keep refreshing it in my heart and mind every day."

Just because you screamed your head off at a concert and lost your voice doesn't mean that you are mature. Ask the Lord right now to fill you with *His* joy. The ride that He takes you on will last forever.

DAY TWO: YOU NEED TO BE FULL OF THE WORD OF GOD
TO STRIKE BACK AT TEMPTATION.

Another sign of immaturity: People who have a hard time standing in the midst of temptation. People can be full of hot air when they
leave a meeting or a camp. They can be thrilled or psyched, but as
soon as any temptation comes along, they get blown over. A mature
person in Christ doesn't do that. It doesn't mean that we're perfect.
It doesn't mean that we never sin or never have temptation. It's not a
sin to be tempted. You're going to be tempted for the rest of your life
(I Corinthians 10:13). The devil is going to take every shot he can at
you. The question is: How are you going to face it when he's tempting you? What are you going to do with that temptation? Are you
going to let him tease you and taunt you with that temptation. Are
you going to barely make it over the hump, sometimes fall, and
sometimes be miserable? Some people feel like that is just the plight
of a Christian. They think there's no way that you can ever really
overcome—you just keep falling and asking for forgiveness.

The Bible says we don't have to live like that. Jesus set a great
example for us when He was being tempted. Read Luke 4:1-13. Look
at it closely and think about some of these questions.

How did Jesus respond every time He was tempted?

_____

_____

_____

_____

_____

_____

You can see that every time the devil gave Jesus a specific temptation, Jesus quoted the Word of God. That is, He didn't go into temptation hoping He would figure out some way to get out. He knew the
Bible well enough so that when the devil came against Him with a
specific thing, He knew exactly how to strike back. You can't strike

back at temptation or the devil by saying, *"You big meany, leave me alone!"* You need to be so full of the Word of God raging on the inside of you that you have a specific Scripture to hit back with when the devil tempts you. Jesus also taught us to pray ...*lead us not into temptation, but deliver us from the evil one.* (Matthew 6:13).

There are two things you can do to fight temptation. You can pray and ask the Lord to keep you from temptation you are not strong enough to resist. The other thing to do is, before temptation comes your way, fill yourself up with the Word of God. Do this especially in areas you know you have problems in—whether that is peer pressure, music, boyfriend/girlfriend situations. Find Scriptures so that when you are tempted you don't get blown over. Getting blown over every time you are tempted, especially with something you have struggled with for a while, is a sign of immaturity. Some people rationalize, *"Well, this is just my weakness, and I'm always going in be weak in this area."* Wrong. The Bible says in Joel 3:10, ...*let the weak say, I am strong.* Areas that you were weak in should become your strongest areas because you get in the Bible and become strong in them.

List your weakest areas right now. These are areas where you most easily get blown over.

_____

_____

_____

_____

_____

_____

Your assignment today is to call people on the phone—your youth pastor, your pastor, anyone you know can help you—and get some Scriptures about these weak areas in your life so you can begin to chew on those Scriptures and get strong.

DAY THREE: IF YOU HAVE A QUIET TIME BUT DON'T DO THINGS TO BUILD YOURSELF UP, YOU'LL GET DISILLUSIONED.

Another sign of immaturity is unfruitful Quiet Times. People start reading their Bibles and praying because they know it is the right thing to do or they heard that other teenagers do it, but soon they find themselves just going through the motions. They read their Bible, shut it, and forget what they read. Or they pray about a couple things that are important to them. For example, *"Lord, please help me to get that new pair of shoes. Lord, please help my hair to get right."* Then they go on with the rest of their day. They think they're doing everything they're supposed to do to be a mature Christian, yet they don't understand why they feel so weak.

Just going through the motions and having a Quiet Time doesn't make you stronger. You have to do the right things in your Quiet Time. If you have a Quiet Time but don't do the right things to really build yourself up, you get the illusion that you're a strong Christian. Just because you're taking 15 minutes or a half hour or an hour every day, you aren't automatically strong. When you do the right things in your Quiet Time, you come out of it feeling like you have pumped iron. You are strong.

Again, people get disillusioned because they feel like they have done everything to get strong but still are not strong. Why keep having Quiet Times? It doesn't do any good to have a Quiet Time if you're not really connecting with God.

You can't just say, *"Well, I read that Bible verse and nothing ever really happened. I read that chapter of Scripture like I do every day and nothing happened."* Instead, you have to take that Word and begin to cram it down your throat like we talked about already—meditate on it, memorize it, chew on it all day long, write it on a card, and take it with you. It's time for serious Christians to stand up and say, *"You know what? I'm tired of going through the motions and pretending I'm mature just because I'm doing this act. I'm only mature if I take what*

I read and apply it to my life and begin to do it." Remember, maturity is not measured just by the things you do or how old you are. It is measured by how obedient you are to do the things that you learn and the things that you read in the Bible.

Think about this, *For the Word of God is living and active. Sharper than any double-edged sword . . .* (Hebrews 4:12).

What does this verse mean to you?

_____

_____

_____

_____

_____

_____

God's Word is living and active, but if you just let it breeze through your brain, it doesn't have enough time to explode and become life on the inside of you.

Take a few minutes to write down some things that you can be doing now in your Quiet Times to make them more useful so that when you leave, you know that you have had a workout.

_____

_____

_____

_____

_____

Commit to do these things starting this morning, starting right now in your Quiet Time.

DAY FOUR: IF YOUR GROWTH IN THE LORD IS DEPENDENT UPON OTHERS, YOU WON'T GROW MUCH.

Another sign of immaturity is relying on others for your spiritual food. Some people are "spiritual leeches." They don't get very much spiritual food, but the food they do get, they get by accident. Maybe God hits them between the eyes when the preacher preached or when a friend said something or when somebody quoted a Scripture. But, they're not growing at all outside of other people's growth. If somebody else grows and talks about it, then they'll grow. However, if they're not around anyone who is growing, they'll stay the same. These spiritually immature Christians often feel like mealy-mouthed helpless little runts who can't do anything for themselves.

How would it be if you were fourteen or fifteen years old and suddenly said, *"Well, I don't really like my food unless somebody else cooks it for me and puts it in my mouth"*? You decide that even though you are fifteen years old you're not eating anything because your mom isn't there to prepare it for you or your dad isn't there to put it on your fork for you. Well, you know that's ridiculous! Yet that's how so many Christians are. It's a sign of immaturity. If your growth in the Lord is totally dependent on other people, then you're never going to grow much. As a strong and growing Christian, you have to take responsibility for your own growth.

The Bible says, *Taste and see that the Lord is good.* (Psalm 34:8). You have to decide to taste it. You have to see that the Lord is good. You have to learn to go get some spiritual food for yourself. You can't feel like it's not really your fault if you don't grow just because you're around people who aren't growing. You can't say *"Well, they didn't feed me very well, or they didn't help me along, or they didn't give me a crutch."* Maybe we don't say it, but we often think it. It is time right now for us to say, *"I'm going to learn. I'll quit relying solely on other people."* Sure, we can learn from their lives and learn from our pastors and parents, but take some responsibility for your own growth.

Take some time now to meditate on Psalm 34:8. Think about what it means to taste for yourself that the Lord is good. Have you been relying only on others to feed you? Commit to the Lord that you will now start taking responsibility for your own growth as a Christian.

DAY FIVE: TO VALUE ONE DAY OVER ANOTHER IS A SIGN OF IMMATURITY.

Another sign of immaturity is if your most spiritual day is Sunday or Wednesday when you go to youth group. You know, some people feel a lot closer to God because they're getting ready to go to church or to youth group that day. They pray more and have better Quiet Times that day figuring it's better to be spiritual on those days than no days at all. This, too, is the sign of a weak Christian. Somehow, in the back of his brain, he thinks that these days are more spiritual or that he needs to look like he's more spiritual on these days than other days. Then on Monday or Tuesday he feels far away from God. He isn't with his Christian friends. He's not motivated to have a good Quiet Time and really live for God with his whole heart on those days. Thursday, Friday, and Saturday, he pretty much takes a vacation from God in his own world. He checks in with God maybe a couple times a week, but only because those are days that he goes to church.

Romans 14:5 says, *One man considers one day more sacred than another; another man considers every day alike. Each one should be fully convinced in his own mind.*

Read Romans 14:1-3. Paul says that if you value one day over another, it is a sign of immaturity. If you are "spiritual" on a specific day because you are supposed to be spiritual on this day, then is your spirituality genuine? If we're really giving our whole life over to God, shouldn't we want to be tight with Him every day? Shouldn't we want to be spiritual every day? Shouldn't we be growing every day?

Take a few minutes to meditate on these verses. Have you been guilty of acting different on some days just because it's the day you go to church? It's time to commit now and say, *"Lord, I'm sorry for acting more spiritual on some days than others. My whole life really does belong to you and I want to be as close as I possibly can to you every day."*

DAY SIX: TRYING TO PLEASE PEOPLE IS GIVING IN TO PEER PRESSURE.

Another sign of spiritual immaturity is trying to look good in front of other Christians instead of just being normal. You know how it is, you are talking with your friends and all of the sudden you see your youth pastor come up, so you change your conversation. What's up with that? Are you doing something that your youth pastor wouldn't be proud of? Then why are you doing it? Don't you realize that you are doing it in front of Jesus whether your youth pastor is there or not? This is a sign that you haven't really grown up much as a Christian. What if you are around some friends at school who aren't saved or are not radical, committed Christians and all of a sudden your friends from youth group come up? Do you mumble the conversation or change the subject? Why is that? Is there something that you're saying to those who aren't saved or those who are half-hearted Christians that you would be ashamed to say in front of people who are really committed? Again, this is a sign of immaturity.

Jesus said, *How can you believe if you accept praise from one another, yet make no effort to obtain the praise that comes from the only God?* (John 5:44). Paul said in Galatians 1:10, *If I were still trying to please men, I would not be a servant of Christ.*

A mature Christian comes to a decision. Who am I going to please? If I believe in Jesus and I've given my life to Him, then He's the one I'm trying to please. Trying to please people around me is giving in to peer pressure. People wouldn't have any problems with peer pressure if they didn't care what other people thought. It is time for us to begin to care more about what God thinks about us than what other people think about us. Peer pressure will affect your spirituality. It will affect whether or not you pray publicly over your food or over your test. It will affect your conversation. It will affect the way you act and what jokes you laugh at when nobody else is around. Our spirituality should not be something that we put on just when "spiritual people" are around us. It is something we pray through every morning before we ever leave our Quiet Time. We commit to God that we are going to act like a spiritual man or woman no matter who else is around because we know He is around all day long.

List some areas right now where you haven't acted very spiritual when other mature believers weren't there:

_____

_____

_____

_____

_____

Commit to pray through everything that you are going to do today. Pray *"Lord, whether there are other mature Christians near me or not, I want to fully represent You because I want to be a mature believer today."*

DAY SEVEN: THESE ARE THE SIGNS OF IMMATURITY.

The last sign of spiritual immaturity is doing things to look good or look spiritual in front of other people who are spiritual. We talked yesterday about doing or saying things that are ungodly. There are other things that we do to try to emphasize our spirituality. When a spiritual person comes around we say, *"Oh, praise the Lord!"* We shout *"Hallelujah!"* or we're always talking about our Quiet Time, or the Bible this or that, or *"God is awesome."* We are saying things to look spiritual on the outside not realizing that we are spiritually hollow. If you find that you're acting this way, it's a mark of immaturity. It's a sign that you're trying to please man instead of God. You are trying to look like something on the outside that you're not on the inside. So much of the Christian life of an immature believer is performance based. In other words, whether he's mature or not he's going to try to look mature to other people. In front of his youth pastor, his Christian parents, or his pastor he's going to say things that look spiritual. He'll be even belligerently "spiritual" to look like he's very tight with God when he really didn't even have a very good Quiet Time that morning.

Matthew 6:1 says, *Be careful not to do your 'acts of righteousness' before men, to be seen by them.* The rest of the chapter talks about specific things we do as Christians—giving, praying, fasting—that mature Christians do all the time, but immature Christians just talk about doing.

It is this fake spirituality that gets us into trouble. Everybody thinks that we're really strong when we aren't. We've even convinced ourselves because we say, *"Praise the Lord, Hallelujah, Glory to God, Amen"* when spiritual people are around. You are not strong just because you say these words. You're strong when you fill yourself up with the Word of God.

Now, review each of the past seven days. Take some of the Scriptures that you have memorized and chew on them again this morning. Take a moment to list below the signs of immaturity. If any of these signs of an immature believer are in your life, circle them.

_____

_____

_____

_____

_____

_____

_____

Now, begin to pray over these things. *"Lord Jesus, I don't want to be all show and nothing real on the inside. I want to develop these areas that look like immaturity in Christ so I can represent You as well as You deserve to be represented in this world. In Jesus Name, Amen."*

CHRISTIANS WITH DIRTY PANTS

DAY ONE: GOD WANTS US TO LEARN HOW TO DEAL WITH SIN.

It's interesting how the family responds when a newborn baby has his first bowel movement. They all stand around, the mother and the father are so proud, they point at it, they look at it, they cheer, *"Look! He had his first stinkies!!"* All kinds of jokes are made about it. Then, as the months go on, people begin to fight over who has to change the baby's diaper—it is no longer a laughing matter. All kinds of excuses are given why each one should not have to change it. The baby-sitters make up reasons why they should not have to change diapers. But the fact is, somebody has to change them. As the baby grows a little bit older, you can see a look of satisfaction on his face after he has filled his diaper to the maximum capacity. He is so happy that there's no more pressure on his stomach. He walks around giving off a horrendous odor but has a big smile on his face, acting like nothing ever happened. Yet, whoever he walks by experiences that undeniable fragrance that gives proof that somebody has filled his pants.

Now when a child is small we might laugh about it or joke about it, but as he grows up a little bit it is no longer a laughing matter. At some point the child is expected to learn how to control himself and not continue to make stinkies in his diapers. If a healthy child were seven years old and still putting stinkies in his diaper, it wouldn't be funny anymore. If he were thirteen years old and still wearing a diaper, smiling every time he filled it, it wouldn't be funny anymore. It would be gross, sick, and pathetic. Yet, that is how so many Christians are.

When somebody first gives his heart to the Lord, he is sure to make mistakes. He thinks, *"Oh well, it was just an accident."* And then he makes another mistake, *"Oh, I just had another accident. . . just had another accident."* Well, if Christians are still having the same kind of "accident" after four and five years of being saved, it's as if they keep filling their pants. In other words, they keep with the same attitudes, or with the same habits, or with the same sins. They walk around just like a baby, acting like nothing is ever wrong. They're rebellious, they have bad attitudes, they're cutting people down, they're lying, cheating, stealing, involved in immorality. Yet, they come to church and act like everything is just fine, but everybody can tell that there is an aroma that they give off. They often cannot even smell it themselves. They say, *"I can't help it. It's just a problem I have."* It's not a problem, it is sin.

Just as it is sick for an older child to have a diaper on and continue to fill it, it's sick to the Lord for us to continue to get ourselves "dirty in sin" over and over and over again. He wants us to learn how to deal with it. He wants us to learn how to control ourselves in the same way a child must learn how to control his bodily functions.

Proverbs 25:28: *Like a city whose walls are broken down is a man who lacks self-control.*

Write out what you think this means

_____

_____

_____

_____

_____

What the Bible is saying here is that if you lack self control it's like you do not have any protection around your life. We continually use the excuse, *"I just can't help it, I can't control myself, it's just a problem I have."* You've no protection against sin. You've not built up a resistance against it. That resistance is like a bulletproof wall to the devil. But if you don't have that wall of resistance, any little temptation or anything that comes your way gets through your shield. It's not good enough for us to say, *" Well, I just can't control myself. It's not really my fault."* You need to start praying about it and learn how to control different parts of your life so you don't walk around as a Christian with dirty pants.

Take a few minutes now and meditate on Proverbs 25:28. Ask the Lord to show you how you can start to build up that wall of protection in your life.

DAY TWO: YOU MUST LEARN HOW TO HAVE SELF-CONTROL.

2 Peter 1:5-6: *For this very reason, make every effort to add to your faith goodness; and to goodness, knowledge; and to knowledge, self-control; and to self-control, perseverance; and to perseverance, godliness.*

Peter gives a perfect progression of growing up. I want to concentrate specifically on *add* to your knowledge, self-control, and *add* to your self-control, perseverance. You're going to learn how to live as a Christian. You're going to begin to get knowledge. As you get knowledge on how you should live, you need to add self-control. In other words, start putting into practice the things that you know are right. It causes you to have self-control.

Now, the Bible wouldn't tell us to have self-control unless the Lord knew that we could. He has given us the power to have control in our life. As we learn the Scriptures and how we should be living, He gives us the power to live that way. Saying you have no self-control is just as ridiculous as saying, *"Well, I can't control my bowels, I can't control whether I go to the bathroom or not."* With a baby that is true, but as that baby grows, he learns to control it even though he didn't know he could. The same is true about you. As God teaches you things from a sermon or a book or from your own Bible study about how you should live, He expects you to take the power of the Holy Spirit that He's put in you and begin to control that area of your life.

Make this commitment with me now: *"In Jesus name, I refuse to keep messing all over myself. I am going to add to what I know, and I'm going to start doing it. I'm going to start forcing my body and my mind and my lips and my life to do what I know is right because I know that I have the power to do it. Then I'm going to add perseverance to my self-control. I'm going to continue to have self-control and do what I know is right. I'm not going to do whatever my body wants to do. I'm not going to do what my sin nature wants to do anymore. Sure that's what I'm naturally prone to do, but that's not what I'm going to do because I know the right things to do now. Just because it's natural, doesn't mean that is what I should do. I have the power to do the right thing. I'm learning to have self-control so that I don't constantly have dirty pants the rest of my life as a Christian."*

Now, I want you to take a moment to write down some of the areas of your life where you need to quit messing on yourself. List the areas you need to start exercising self-control in.

_____

_____

_____

_____

_____

_____

_____

_____

Now pray over these and say, *"Lord, in Jesus name, I commit these areas to you. I no longer want to be getting myself dirty in sin in all these areas of my life. I am going to start living and doing what I know is right. In Jesus name, Amen."*

DAY THREE: THE FRUIT OF THE SPIRIT IS SELF-CONTROL.

Galatians 5:22,23: *The fruit of the spirit is love, joy, peace, patience, kindness, goodness, faithfulness, gentleness, and self-control. Against such things there is no law.*

We were talking about growing in the Lord and not being a baby in the things of Christ anymore. Today's Scripture begins, *"the fruit of the spirit."* Note that *"fruit"* does not just appear on trees. You don't walk out to an apple tree one day and see blossoms and the next day see apples. The apples have to grow. First the blossom turns into a seed, which develops into a small apple, which grows into a large apple, which finally ripens. This is the same thing that God wants to do in our life. We pray, *"Cause me to mature so I grow fruit."* You don't just pray for the fruit of the spirit, *"God make me patient, God make me kind, God make me loving, God give me self-control, give it to me now."* To mature and grow up as a Christian you must pursue making the fruit grow.

If fruit is going to grow, the seed must be planted, watered, and fertilized. The seed is the Word of God. You plant it in your heart. You begin to learn it, chew on it, meditate on it. You water it: by partaking in praise and worship, cultivating a humble heart, and adding to your knowledge. You keep learning more and more about the Lord so you can continue to exercise self-control in the areas you learn about.

The fruit of the spirit is self-control. Begin to demand that you do what you learn about. Picture yourself as a fruit tree, growing the fruit of the Spirit and constantly pursuing maturity and growth. You are not somebody with just a bunch of blossoms, as a lot of Christians are. You don't have just a lot of little baby fruit. Work to grow mature, healthy, plump, juicy fruit on your tree. When people get around you they say, *"Wow, you have really grown."* Those who see you from one month or from one year to the next will see a lot of growth in your life. In areas where you used to be impatient, you're really patient. In areas where you used to be really rebellious, you're really submissive. Take a moment here and list some areas in your life that, over the next two months, you want people to look at you and say, *"Wow, I see growth in this area:"*

_____

_____

_____

_____

_____

_____

_____

_____

Pray over these areas right now. Say, *"Lord, in Jesus name, these are the areas I want to grow in. I don't want to just stay the same. I don't want to make up excuses why I am still looking like I have immature fruit or no growth in my life in these areas. In Jesus name, as I learn what Your Word says about these, I promise to apply self-control over my sinful nature so that You can be glorified in the way I live. In Jesus name, Amen."*

Now take five minutes and memorize Galatians 5:22,23. Meditate on these verses as you begin to work on getting mature fruit in your life.

DAY FOUR: TAKE CONTROL AND REPENT OF FILTHY LANGUAGE.

Let's talk about some of the specific areas that immature Christians are constantly "dirtying themselves" in. First we'll talk about our language or the way we talk. This world is so corrupt and corroded in the way people talk to each other and the way they refer to other people. Not just the cussing and swearing, but slamming people and stabbing them in the back.

Colossians 3:8: *But now you must rid yourselves of all such things as these: anger, rage, malice, slander, and filthy language from your lips.*

It says, . . . *rid yourselves of . . . filthy language.* Think about filthy language. It's not just swearing. It's having garbage coming out of your mouth. Whether it's garbage jokes, garbage cutting other people down, or garbage in the way you refer to leaders, it's just filthy language that's not honoring to God. You might say, *"Well, I just can't help it,"* but the good news is that you *can* help it. Now that you know that filthy language shouldn't be coming out of your mouth, add self-control to your knowledge. You say, *"In Jesus name, I am going to take control over my tongue."*

Another area of filthy language is lying. Don't say things that are untrue, whether it's what we call "white lies" or it's blatant lies to our mom and dad. It's time for us to become people of truth. You know you don't have to lie. You might have a particular propensity to lie because that's the way you learned how to get away with things. But as a new creation, as a man or woman of God, there needs to be new words on your lips saying, *"I'm going to be a person of truth and do what is right, controlling my tongue."* I want you to list a couple of ways you want to begin to correct the way you talk. This is the first step to clean up and "change your diapers" in the way that you talk.

_____

_____

_____

_____

"Change your diapers." What that really means is to repent. When you find a certain area in your life, the way you get clean and take control is to repent. You say, *"In Jesus name, I am not going to talk like that anymore. Lord I repent of talking like this. I repent of using the tongue that You have given me to let this garbage come out of my mouth. I choose to use self-control and submit this area of my life to You. In Jesus name, Amen."*

Now, I want you to take Colossians 3:8 with you all day long. First, take the next few minutes and meditate on it. Then, use it all day long to renew your mind and the way you think. Use it to give you power as you chew on it. Write it down, take it with you, use it all day long. Then if you are tempted today to use your tongue for garbage, let this verse will come out of your mouth instead. You choose to use self-control, you choose to have this Scripture come out instead of the garbage you were about to say.

Have a great day!

DAY FIVE: YOU HAVE THE POWER TO AVOID SEXUAL IMMORALITY.

Let's talk about immorality. Children dirty their pants, and Christians make huge mistakes and then try to justify them away. Now if you're in a nursery hanging out with a bunch of children and they all dirty their pants, it is easier to say, *"Well, mine don't smell that bad because everybody else's smells, too."* But, if you're twelve years old and hanging around a bunch of other people who are not in the nursery and you're dirtying your pants, you can tell that it smells pretty bad.

It's the same way with immorality. If you are hanging around a bunch of other worldly people who are fooling around with sex a lot, but you're not *too* much, then you feel pretty righteous about it. You don't seem to smell *too* bad. But if you are hanging out with people who are really going after God and you blow it just a little bit, you're going to realize it smells pretty bad to them and to the Lord because it's messing up your life.

The Bible has a lot to say about fleeing immorality. I Corinthians 6:18 says, *Flee from sexual immorality. All other sins a man commits are outside his body, but he who sins sexually sins against his own body.* Ephesians 5:3 says, *But among you there must not be even a hint of sexual immorality,* not even a look or an attitude, looking at a girl up and down, or checking out a guy's body.

Colossians 3:5: *Put to death, therefore, whatever belongs to your earthly nature: sexual immorality, impurity, lust, evil desires and greed, which is idolatry.* Note here that it says to put it to death. That means change your diapers. Don't think like that, don't act like that, don't do that thing anymore. I Thessalonians 4:3: *It is God's will that you should be sanctified: that you should avoid sexual immorality.* It says, *avoid sexual immorality.* You have the power to steer around it. You don't have to keep messing your pants and saying, *"But I just can't help it."* Yes, you can help it. Keep the lights on, stay out of the dark, stay away from being alone with a guy or a girl. The good news is that God has given you the power to have self-control.

I want you to think right now of any sexual immorality you may have in your life, now or in the past. Include thoughts or anything that could have been interpreted as a hint of sexual immorality. Take a moment now to pray and repent. *"God, I'm sorry. I want to be totally clean, and I choose to use self-control in this area of my life."* Take three minutes to meditate on I Corinthians 6:18 right now.

Now, take four minutes to meditate on Ephesians 5:3. Say it over and over and over and over again until it starts getting down in your heart. Now take these two Scriptures today; memorize them, chew on them. Make them a part of you so that any time you get tempted with any thought of immoral action you're ready. Instead of following through with that action (or even just continuing to think on that thought), rip these Scriptures out as an act of self-control. You don't do this because you feel like it, but you force yourself to remember the right way, the godly way, the honorable way to respond.

Changing your dirty pants in this area means repenting and saying, *"Lord, I refuse to just do what my body or what society says is the norm to do. I am going to do the right thing. To make sure I remember the right thing, I am going to cram these Bible verses down into my heart so that it is my natural response the next time I am tempted."* It's the natural response when you feel like you have to go to the bathroom to run to the bathroom, even in the middle of the night. In the same way, your natural response when you are tempted with immorality should be to run to the Scripture. Rip it out of your heart. Rip it out of your pocket and quote that thing so it becomes natural for you to have clean diapers.

DAY SIX: GOD'S HIGH IS BETTER THAN THE HIGH ALCOHOL CAN GIVE YOU.

Let's talk about drinking now. The Bible says in Ephesians 5:18: *Do not get drunk on wine, which leads to debauchery.* Write this verse out in modern teenage words.

_____

_____

_____

_____

_____

_____

_____

_____

If this is an area you have been filling your diapers in, if drinking and getting drunk is one of those things you have continually messed up on, it's time for you to get a handle on it. It doesn't matter if drinking has been something you've been around your whole life. It doesn't matter if your family drinks or not, you don't have to be a slave to drinking anymore. Some people feel that because their families had a problem with drinking that they're just doomed to give in to it. Or they think that because all their friends drink or that's the way they've always lived, they're just always going to be involved with drinking. You need to understand that the Bible says you have the power and the authority to live free from that. Besides, the high that God gives you is way better than the high that any beer or whiskey could give you. Man, don't get full of the world; get filled with the Holy Spirit, get full of God. Let God invade every part of your life.

If alcohol has been a temptation for you, or if this has been a problem in the past, you need to grab a hold of the Scripture and cram it down inside of you. You need to get rid of your dirty pants in this area and say, "*You know what, I am not going to put up with this any more. I am not going to act like this is just some little problem I have. This is a sin, it's messing me up, and I'm going to put it down once and for all and say: No more will I allow this area to rule over me. Next time I feel like I want to grab a beer, or go to a party, instead of reaching for a beer, I am going reach for the Word of God. I am going to reach for this Scripture and I am going to let it come out of my mouth.*"

Remember, the Word of God is sharp. It is living and active, sharper than any two-edged sword. It will make you sharp. It will make you strong because it will fill you with the power of God as you continue to meditate on it. Write Ephesians 5:18 on a card and take it with you all day if this is an area in life you need to repent of. It is time to grow up. Quit making excuses in your life, and say, "*In Jesus name, I'm going to quit messing my pants in this area. I'm too old, I'm too strong, I've been around God too long to keep walking around filling my pants with this garbage, filling my life with this garbage and acting like it's just another problem. It's time for me to grow up.*"

If drinking is not a problem area for you, then make a commitment now that you'll never even get started. Promise yourself now that you'll stay pure and free from drinking for the rest of your life.

DAY SEVEN: DON'T BE A CHRISTIAN WITH DIRTY PANTS.

There are so many other areas that we could talk about, other things that you may have dirtied your life with, or areas of that need cleaning up. Maybe stealing is something you struggle with. For you there is Ephesians 4:28: *He who has been stealing must steal no longer, but must work, doing something useful with his own hands, that he may have something to share with those in need.*

For every sin that you have had a problem with, that messed up your life, or polluted your life with garbage there is a Scripture to deal with it. Instead of saying, *"Okay, I'll do mind over matter and try to get over this,"* say, *"I'm going to find the Scripture that has to do with this sin issue I'm dealing with, and I refuse to just try to be a better person. I'm going to deal with these specific areas. I'm going to quit walking around like a baby with dirty diapers."*

I want to encourage you to look back over the week. Look at all the different Scriptures we have used and those Scriptures you have meditated on this week. Spend a few minutes now reviewing those Scriptures that you've memorized. Write the references here for the verses you are especially going to concentrate on in the coming weeks.

_____

_____

_____

_____

_____

_____

Decide right now that you are going to learn how to change your own diapers, and that nobody has to convince you that you really do have dirty diapers. Most of the time, that's what revival and camps are all about: trying to convince you that you have sin in your life so you will repent. But as a mature believer I don't have to be convinced. I know if I have dirt in my diapers. Man, I know if I'm sinning. I'm not going to walk around with a hard heart waiting until it gets stinking so bad that it's obvious to the whole world before I repent. At the first little sign of a smell, I'm going to get that smell out of my life. Then I'm going to learn how to control my life so that I don't keep sinning and messing up in the same area again and again for the rest of my life.

Remember, it's not cute if you're a teenager and you're still filling your diapers. I's not cute if you're walking around with a bunch of garbage sin in your life that you should have grown out of by now. You grow out of it by finding Scriptures that deals with that specific sin and then memorizing them, meditating on them, cramming them down your throat until your natural reaction is not to do that sin, but your natural reaction is to grab that Scripture and fight off temptation the same way Jesus did.

ACTION POINTS

What am I going to do in response to what I learned this week?

_____

_____

_____

_____

_____

_____

_____

_____

_____

_____

_____

_____

WEEK FOUR

....

IT IS TIME TO GET OFF THE BOTTLE

DAY ONE: DO YOU REALLY CRAVE THE FOOD OF THE WORD OF GOD?

When babies are born they have to eat. Whether they're breast fed or bottle fed, they must have milk to live. They can't get food on their own; they have to get it from their parents. As they grow and continue to mature they start eating soft food out of a jar. As they develop teeth they can have little bits of chunks in that food. As they get a full set of teeth, they can have food that is more solid. We have all seen the progression.

What happens when a youngster is in a high chair trying to learn how to eat? He thinks he can feed himself before his parents think he can. He demands to feed himself and ends up getting food all over his face. He throws it on the floor and across the kitchen. Of course, the goal is that at some point he learns how to get that food into his mouth and actually chew it and get it down into his stomach. There are all kinds of jokes and family stories of how mishaps have happened at the table, something spilled in the middle of an important dinner or food was thrown hitting somebody in the face. People laugh and joke about how youngsters throw their food onto the floor or smear it all over their face, but after a time it is not funny anymore.

There is a certain age between two and three years old when the child is expected to learn how to feed himself and not make such a big mess. If he is nine or ten years old and still throwing food on the floor, smearing food all over his face, and throwing food at others, it is no longer funny. It's a nuisance, and it's rebellion. What if he were fifteen or sixteen years old and still smooshing food all over his face and still had not learned how to get it down? Is he still saying, *"Mommy, Daddy, come feed me." "Mommy, Daddy, come put it on a fork for me and put it in my mouth."* Or, *"I do not like it like this."* Or, *"I want it hot."* Or, *"I want it cold."* Well, then it shows that he has not grown up. He has not matured.

Many Christians are like these children who have not learned to feed themselves yet. They sit in church their whole life demanding that their pastor or youth pastor feeds them. They can't get any food for themselves. When they do get food from a great sermon preached to them, they listen to part of it and throw part of it on the floor. Or they smash it on their face and talk about it for a week, but they really do not digest it. They do not really put into their life.

As young Christians we need to be fed. As baby Christians we need milk, but there comes a time when we need to learn how to eat meatier, solid foods. Then there comes a time after eating solid food that we need to learn how to feed ourselves and not be sucking on the bottle at church every week. We need to dive into the Word of God for ourselves to get meat.

The Bible says in I Peter 2:2: *Crave spiritual milk, so that by it you may grow up in your salvation.* Do you really crave it? Now you know little babies crave milk. They long for it, and they cry when they don't get it. They just have to have it. Are you that hungry for God? Do you crave it? Do you want it? Do you say, *"Oh, God, feed me"*? Do you go to church saying, *"Oh, Lord, feed me"*? Do you tell to your youth pastor, your pastor, your parents, *"Please teach me more. I want to grow, I want to grow"*? The first issue here is, do you really crave the food of the Word of God? Do you crave spiritual milk, spiritual nutrition? If you don't, that's the issue that needs to be dealt with. If you don't want to eat, if you don't feel like you are hungry, you need to repent and get hungry. Most people aren't craving God's Word when they go to church, they just go out of tradition. If you're so full of the world—that is full of busyness, movies, secular music—then you won't have any more room for anything else. You won't even realize that you have a spiritual hunger inside. But when you do the stuff that we did last week, when you repent and get your diapers and your heart all clean, then you're going to realize you have to get yourself filled up. If you don't have a real craving for spiritual milk, for spiritual nutrition, then ask God to break your heart this week. Ask God to fill you with a supernatural craving, a ravenous desire for food and nutrition, for the Word of God.

Take three minutes right now and meditate on 1 Peter 2:2. Take it with you today and all week long. Then, start chewing on it. Say, *"Lord, I want to crave spiritual milk. Lord, I want to grow. I have to have spiritual nutrition."* Chew on it until a spiritual hunger begins to explode inside of you.

DAY TWO: IF ALL WE CAN HANDLE IS MILK, THAT'S ALL WE'RE GOING TO GET.

I Corinthians 3:2: *I gave you milk, not solid food, for you were not yet ready for it. Indeed, you are still not ready.* Paul is saying, *"Listen, I wanted you guys to grow. I really wanted you to get solid food, but you guys are still acting like babies so I can only give you milk."* God wants to give us solid food. He wants to give us the deep stuff, the stuff that no one else has ever understood. People who have been in church their whole lives have just been sucking on milk, but God has been wanting to fill them with solid food from His Word. He wants them to understand how to live, to grow, to prosper, and to change the world. He wants to show you how to make not just a little dent in your school, but a total revolution. He wants to show you that deep stuff. He wants to show you incredible, amazing stuff. But if we are still so immature that all we can handle is milk, then that is all we are going to get.

People who have gone to church for years may think, *"Oh, I have heard that sermon before."* It is all milk, milk, milk, because they've never had enough guts to really grow up. They haven't made the effort to learn the milk, to apply it to their lives, and to do it so that God can trust them with more. People pray, *"Oh God, I want to change the world, I want to change my whole school."* If they don't do anything with the milk God has been giving them, He is not going to give them solid food.

Babies must quit drinking milk after a while and go on to chew on solid food. So it is with Christians. After a while you should have learned that Jesus really did forgive all your sins, so why are you still living with them? Jesus really does want you to become victorious and quit having dirty diapers, so why are you still having them? You have to get beyond the milk and get the essentials down. Start living clean, living free, living holy so you can go on. If you really want to get the deep stuff, if you want to get the solid food, you have to apply the spiritual milk to your life.

Begin now by spending the next five minutes meditating on I Corinthians 3:2. Memorize it, and think about what it means. Ask God to show you how this verse could begin today to change the rest of your life.

DAY THREE: SOLID FOOD IS FOR THE MATURE CHRISTIAN.

Hebrews 5:14 says, *Solid food is for the mature, who by constant use have trained themselves to distinguish good from evil.* One of the signs that a baby is starting to grow up is that he can have solid foods. One of the signs of maturity in the Lord is your response to the meat. How do you respond when someone gives you a piece of solid food? When you hear a sermon or someone confronts you about something in your life, like having a real subtle attitude or not treating people with love or respect, how do you respond? Some people get away with those things all the time, but not you. Because you want solid food you're not dealing with big immorality kinds of sins, like murder or getting drunk all the time. You have a piece of meat that's talking about your envious heart. Instead of getting defensive you say, *"Wait a minute, I want to be mature about this. I want to take that piece of solid food and apply it to my life, I want to deal with this area of my life."*

List here some areas where you have been confronted, either in person or in a sermon. Describe how you responded and how you could have responded better.

_____

_____

_____

_____

_____

_____

_____

_____

Solid food is for the mature. One of the signs of maturity is really wanting to eat and wanting to eat solid food. The mature will deal with any area of their life, even if others are not having to deal with it. You may not hear sermons on these issues all the time, but you may read something in the Scripture or hear somebody saying something in a sermon or in a conversation with you. Instead of getting defensive, take that solid food and chew on it, and chew on it, and chew on it until you digest it and get it into your heart and into your life.

Now take three minutes to memorize and meditate on Hebrews 5:14. Get it so deep in your heart that the next time you hear a sermon you will recognize the meat in it and be able to apply that meat to your life.

DAY FOUR: IF YOU WANT TO GROW UP, YOU MUST START FEEDING YOURSELF.

Let's talk about why people don't feed themselves. First of all, a baby can't feed herself. She drinks milk or whatever she can get. So if you are a brand new Christian, don't get a big guilt trip over this. Just get around whatever kind of good spiritual nutrition you can possibly get. Go to church, listen to tapes, fill yourself up, apply it to your life, and keep pouring that Scripture into yourself. A good place to start is the Scripture 1 Peter 2:2, *crave spiritual milk,* that you have been meditating on all week.

There are other reasons people don't feed themselves, though. One reason is they like others to wait on them, like a little two-year-old baby who is saying, *"Mama, give me this. Mama, give me that."* That is what a lot of Christians would like. They keep saying, *"Pastor, give it to me this way. No, I don't like it that way."* Or, *"I don't like the way he preaches."* Or, *"I don't like what that sermon was about."* These are the people who always have a commentary on the pastor's sermon. These are the people who are always mocking the youth pastor—the way he preaches, or an illustration or a story he uses. They don't pay attention to the content. They pay more attention to the messenger than the message. They pay attention to the personality rather than what the person is saying that could change their life. It's a mark of immaturity. They take what they're served, and because they don't like it, they throw it on the floor like a two year old. So they don't eat. They take the Word of God that others are trying to plant into their lives so they can grow and get mature, and they throw it on the floor. They say they don't like the way it tastes. They don't like the way the pastor said it. They don't like his attitude. Even if you don't like the speaker at all and you are personally offended by him, if he's giving you the Word of God you can get something to grow with out of that sermon. A mature person will do that.

Another reason people don't eat is they are just plain lazy. They're too lazy to put the spoon into the bowl and bring it up into their mouth. Sometimes our little boy is like that. He has the ability, I know he can do it, but sometimes he just says, *"No, I want Mama to do it."* Or, *"I want Papa to do it."* This is how a lot of Christians live. They have the ability to feed themselves, but they don't want to. They want somebody else to dive into the Word of God. They want somebody else to put a three-point sermon together with nice little illustrations and some funny jokes. That's the only way they will eat. The fact is they're just lazy. They don't want to do word studies and find ways to get an understanding of what the Bible is really trying to say. They won't take the time to pull out their dictionary or other books to help them learn. As a result of their laziness, they never grow. List some of the reasons you haven't been growing.

_____

_____

_____

_____

_____

_____

_____

This may sound harsh, but it is true. If you want to grow up, it's time to start feeding yourself. The food that you're fed, eat with gratefulness. Thank God for it, and learn how to get nutrition out of it. But it's time to learn to grow up and feed yourself. If you've been lazy, it's time to quit! Take a few minutes to review Hebrews 5:14. Start getting that solid food and feeding yourself.

DAY FIVE: MAKE IT A LIFELONG PASSION TO FEED YOUR-SELF.

We're talking about learning how to feed ourselves. You need to grow up so you're not living like a leech all the time, but instead you're learning how to feed yourself. Let's talk about some practical things.

How can you feed yourself? The first thing, and I know this sounds basic, is read the Bible. Don't just read it in a casual way. Don't read it just to pass the time. Don't just read it out of obligation. Read it to really learn. Before you start to read say, *"Lord, I'm craving spiritual milk today. Lord, I want you to feed me. Fill me up today, Lord."* Then open your Bible and read. Read through several Scriptures, maybe a whole chapter, maybe ten or so verses. Then go back and ask yourself some questions. *"What is God really trying to say in this passage?" "What is God saying to me about my life in this passage?"*

Now, before we go any further, I want you to practice this. Find a Scripture passage that you have been reading in the Bible. Write it here:

_____

_____

_____

_____

_____

_____

Now what is the Lord trying to say to you through this passage?

_____

_____

_____

_____

_____

_____

Now pray about this area of your life where God is speaking to you. Say, *"Lord, I am going to take this passage and apply it to my life today. I am going to take it into my heart. I'm not just going to be a hearer of Your Word. I am going to do it today, in Jesus name."*

We've already been talking about and practicing other ways to feed yourself. We've talked about taking Scriptures and memorizing them and meditating on them. When you do that you feed your spirit man and build your faith. Somebody says, *"Well, that's too hard, I don't want to do that."* Or, *"I've done that before."* Now first of all, meditating is not the same as memorizing. Memorizing is the first step. Meditation is where you get the real nutrition. So if you think, *"Well, Okay. I'm just going to memorize like I did my memory verses when I was a child,"* then you won't get the real thunder out of this. You won't get the real value out of it. All you have is a nice little Scripture you are chanting. So you say, *"That's too hard; I don't want to do that."* Is it really so hard, just memorizing and meditating on a Scripture? Is it harder than living in sin? Is it harder than being frustrated with the same thing, over and over and over again? Is it harder than living as a spiritual baby? Would you rather be bored with God your whole life because you never had enough courage to dive into the Bible? You need to say, *"I'm going to meditate on this. I'm going to chew on it. I'm going to grow. I'm going to apply this to my life."*

It's time to make a commitment to start feeding yourself. Start getting into the Scripture. Meditate on and memorize the Scriptures that are in this book, and keep finding other Scriptures. Make this a lifelong passion to feed yourself and not walk around like a sniveling little baby if somebody doesn't preach just right. Begin to feed yourself the Word of God.

DAY SIX: AS A YOUNG PERSON WHO LOVES GOD, YOU SHOULD HUNGER, THIRST, AND CRAVE THAT PURE, SPIRITUAL MILK.

We are going to continue to talk about how to feed yourself. What can you do to feed yourself? Of course, we learned yesterday about learning the Word of God and how we can use that to feed ourselves. But there are a number of other things as well. 2 Timothy 2:15 says, *Study to show thyself approved unto God, a workman that needeth not to be ashamed, rightly dividing the word of truth.*

When you go to church, take notes on the sermons that you hear, both from your youth pastor and from your pastor. Don't just sit there like a bump on a log. Chew on the meat they give you. I've preached to people all around the world—preached live to hundreds of thousands of people, seen hundreds of thousands of people saved, been on national TV on a regular basis—but every time I sit through a service I have a pen in my hand and I'm ready to write. You see, if I hear something that really strikes my heart I don't want to forget it. I'm going to chew on it. Then later I'll go back to it and study it more.

Find Christian books like this one and others that will help you grow. Note other areas in your life that you need to grow in, where you need to get rid of the dirty diapers in your life, and find books dealing with those issues. When you read those books, don't simply read through them. Highlight different areas, write things down, take notes in your journal or in the back of your Bible. Write down everything that you really want to remember. You should be constantly devouring Christian books. At any given time, I'm reading five or six books. When I finish a book, then I start another. I have several books going at a time because I want to grow in a number of different areas of my life. It's called feeding yourself. It's developing and growing up as a Christian.

Listening to Christian tapes is a great way to grow. Listening to sermons is good. Don't just listen to Christian music tapes. Listen to worship tapes as well as teaching tapes. If you do listen to contemporary Christian music, listen to the lyrics and find out about the artist. Try to learn something from the lyrics that will help you grow rather than just passively listening to them because of a cool song. Find something that has incredible lyrics that could help you to grow. It may not be the coolest song, but it might just be like a mini power-packed sermon that could change your life. Also, listen to preaching tapes. This shouldn't be something just adults do. As a young person who loves God, you're hungering and thirsting and craving that pure spiritual milk. Listen to sermons and take notes just like you would if you were listening to your pastor. Put those notes in your journal and meditate on them so that you can grow up as a man or woman of God.

Watch videos. Watch videos of preaching and other Christian videos that will stimulate your growth, stimulate your perspective on life, and help you to grow up (the movie *Jesus* is a good one). Be hungry and take notes on what you learn. Help to feed the hunger that you have for God.

DAY SEVEN: IT'S TIME TO GET OFF THE BOTTLE.

Take a few minutes now and review all the Scriptures we've used this week. Review the things that we've talked about as far as craving spiritual milk and growing up in the Lord. Think about what you've learned about feeding yourself and not acting like a baby, not throwing your food around. Make some lifelong decisions today as a result of all you've learned this week. What are you going to do to make sure that you're not one of those spoiled-brat kids who still don't know how to feed themselves at the age of three or four years old?

I want to encourage you to make a plan right now. Make a plan of how you are going to continually feed yourself. Make your plan specific, such as: every week I am going to take notes, I'm going to listen to *"x"* many tapes a week, I'm going to read *"x"* many books about the Lord every six months. Don't just say, *"Well, I'll be Joe Spiritual."'* Make plans to grow up as a Christian, to become mature. Get off the milk and get on solid food. Learn how to feed yourself. Determine to memorize *"x"* many Scriptures a week and meditate on them.

Your plan may be way more than what your friends or other Christians you know are doing. It has nothing to do with whether you are more or less spiritual than others. What's important is *are you as spiritual as God wants you to be? Are you growing at the rate that He wants you to grow?* It's not an option, it's just a matter of spiritual survival. If you want to grow up and quit struggling with the same areas of sin that you've always dealt with, then digest the food you're getting and learn how to feed yourself.

Take a few minutes now to pray and then write out some steps you will take to become more of who God wants you to be. What is your plan?

Maybe you could make a page for this in your journal or in the back of your Bible so you can add to it as you get more ideas from God and so you can keep track as you begin to meet some of your goals.

ACTION POINTS

What am I going to do in response to what I learned this week?

_____

_____

_____

_____

_____

_____

_____

_____

_____

_____

_____

_____

_____

_____

WEEK FIVE

....

LEARNING TO STAND AND WALK

DAY ONE: GOD NEEDS CHRISTIANS TO START LIVING LIKE CHRISTIANS.

There's a time in a baby's life, as she is crawling all over the house, and then she notices that her parents, that brothers, and sisters are not crawling around at all. She sees they are on two feet and walking. A light comes on and the baby says, *"Hey, I need to stand up. I need to walk."* She begins to get a look of determination in her eyes as she scoots up next to a couch and tries to pull herself up. Her little muscles strain and shake under the weight of her body. This is not just another good idea to this baby, it's an imperative. She'll do whatever it takes to get herself up on two feet.

Sure, it's cute to watch babies crawl around the house and do somersaults and other cute things that babies do, but there comes a time when crawling isn't cute anymore. If they were still crawling at eight years old, nobody would be saying how cute that was.

Too many Christians have been crawling their whole life. They have never stood up on two feet or learned to walk. They have never taken responsibility for their own spiritual growth or for their own spiritual strength. The fact is, many Christians don't really want to get up and walk. Isn't it amazing that a tiny baby could have a stronger desire to get up and walk than most Christians? Is their determination to stand stronger than our determination to live for God? We are all capable of that kind of resolve. We all started out just like that baby. The problem is many Christians don't even know they should want to stand. They don't know they should start walking as a strong man or woman of God. They think they're doomed to keep falling and stay weak Christians.

When an athlete is preparing for a winning game or a championship, he has to be completely focused. With all his energy he has to really want to win. He has to want to be the best. His heart drives him to be the best and to practice at his highest skill, at the level of a champion. It all starts in his heart, and it's the same in our Christian life. How much do you want to walk? How seriously do you want to be strong? How much do you want to be free from sin? You may say, *"Well, I have a weakness in this particular area."* Or *"I'm not very strong here."* But it all starts in your heart. When coaches of championship ball teams are asked the most important ingredient in a good player, they say it again and again, *"it's the heart, it's not the skill level."* Many people are born with natural skill but don't have heart so they never develop themselves to their full potential.

I believe it's the same way in Christianity. Young people raised in church have a natural tendency to do Christian things. But they often don't have a heart that really desires to compete and to grow. They don't have the spirit and determination to get up and walk.

I John 1:7: *But if we walk in the light, as he is in the light, we have fellowship with one another, and the blood of Jesus, his Son, purifies us from all sin.* What does it really mean to walk in the light as He is in the light? God needs Christians to start living like Jesus. How desperately do you want to live like Him? If you need to, ask the Lord to change your heart. If you're finding that a spirit of determination is not in you, maybe you're over-familiarized with Christianity. Are you like that athlete born with natural talent but who doesn't have the heart to really want to win a championship. Do you know the things to do, but don't have the drive to really want to grow? Ask God to change your heart. Ask Him to give you the heart of a child to really want to get up and walk.

Take three minutes right now to memorize 1 John 1:7. Write it on an index card and carry it with you all day today. Pull it out throughout the day today and meditate on it.

DAY TWO: TO GET UP AND WALK, YOU HAVE TO VIOLATE YOUR NATURAL TENDENCY TO SIN.

It's time to start pulling yourself up. You're beginning to get a heart to want to walk. It's important to go through the process of getting up to walk just like a baby does. The first thing you need to realize is that it is going to be tough work. You have to learn to pull yourself up. In your Christian walk, that means pulling yourself out of the world. You have to pull yourself out of ungodly habits, away from ungodly friends, out of lukewarm Christianity. You have to pull yourself up.

This, too, is like an athlete in training. As the Bible says, *Everyone who competes in the games goes into strict training.* (I Corinthians 9:25) An athlete who really wants to win knows he's going to have to work hard. As he prepares for the game, he can't just pray for it, hope for it, ask for it, or just get on the right team. He's going to have to work hard for it himself. He is going to have to exercise his muscles. He is going have to work harder than the average person if he wants to be more than an average athlete. In the same way, you're going to have to work harder if you want to be more than an average Christian. You have to pull yourself up. You have to learn to push hard against your flesh and not do what your natural tendencies tell you to do.

If you're going to get up and walk, you're going to have to violate your natural inclination to sin. You can't afford to be a lazy person and a lazy Christian. You're going to have to sweat a little bit. You can't just talk about sweat. You can't just want to sweat. You have to sweat.

What does it mean to sweat in your Christianity? You sweat by memorizing and meditating on Scripture. You sweat by not doing what you really, really want to do in your flesh but know is just not right in your spirit. When you say no to that thing, you are pulling yourself up. How much do you want to compete? If you want to stand up and walk, it's time to start sweating. Meditate on I Corinthians 9:25 all day today.

What are some areas where you need to pull yourself out of? Write them here and then ask God to help you be strong.

_____

_____

_____

_____

_____

_____

_____

_____

DAY THREE: YOU HAVE TO WORK AT STANDING.

Ephesians 6:13: *After you have done everything, to stand.* After you pull yourself up, it's time for you to learn how to balance. It's time to stand up. At first an adult needs to help a child learn to stand. Several times he must help her get up, but after a while she is expected to learn how to balance for herself and stand.

The problem is that many Christians have never learned how to stand. They barely get up and they think they're a spiritual tower of strength. When a little temptation comes, they get blown over. Then they get discouraged wondering if they can even get up again. In the same way a parent helps his child get his balance, we need our youth pastors, our pastors, and our parents to help us stand spiritually at first. But when a healthy child is ten years old, it is not cute for him to be holding onto his mom's or dad's leg just to keep balance.

That is what many Christians have done. They are like leeches sucking the life out of anybody who is around them. They rely on others to keep them balanced. Instead of learning how to plant their feet and stand firm like the Bible talks about, they rely on others to keep them standing. Jesus fully expects us to get our own footing and to stand firm ourselves. When your feet are established in the Word of God and a temptation tries to blow you over, it can't knock you over because you're stronger than the temptation. The things that you learned last week, the Scripture you applied to your life, gave you a firm foundation to stand on so you are not easily frayed or blown over. Don't think that the only people who need to be that strong are our pastors. If you expect them to be the only really strong ones, you'll get disillusioned if they fall or get into sin. It should be all Christians who are serious about God and learn to stand.

You don't stand by just telling yourself, *"Oh, I want to stand, I want to stand."* You have to work, you have to pull yourself up. As we talked about yesterday, it's very important to meditate on the Scripture. You have to read it and chew on it repeatedly. Having God's Word in your heart helps you to stand when the world wants to blow you over. That's why I've given you so many Scriptures to meditate on and memorize in this book. They'll help you stand and keep you strong when everybody else gets blown over. Write out some of the Scriptures we've talked about that you can use to stand strong.

_____

_____

_____

_____

_____

_____

_____

Take Ephesians 6:13 today and chew on it all day long. Meditate on it and learn to stand today.

DAY FOUR: LEARNING TO WALK SPIRITUALLY TAKES DETERMINATION.

3 John 3: *It gave me great joy to have some brothers come and tell about your faithfulness to the truth and how you continue to walk in the truth.* After a child learns to stand, he'll launch into the deep to take his first few steps, the first few steps out of millions he'll take in his life. Learning to walk takes an incredible amount of determination just like learning to pull up did. Learning to walk spiritually takes the same amount of determination. Learning to walk spiritually is essentially putting into practice what you have learned about God. You have heard the expression, "He talks the talk, but he doesn't walk the walk." This expression is referring to hypocrites. It means they can talk about Christianity, but they don't live it. They have a lot of hot air, but they don't ever live what they're talking about. Too many modern Christians fall into that category.

When a child learns to walk she holds onto her parents' fingers. Her parents are helping her learn how to take each step. That's exactly what we need to do when we first learn how to walk out our Christianity. We need our pastors, parents, and youth pastors to help us to walk. They will help us learn how to apply godly principles to our life so that we're not just talking, but we're actually doing what we're talking about. Even as a child who's learning to walk wants his parents to keep helping him, we get used to holding onto our leaders. We don't want to let go. We get used to being in the "walker," you know that saucer-on-wheels that helps a child learn how to walk. Then we don't ever want to get out. We feel safe as long as somebody is holding us up, holding on to us, and walking with us. Unfortunately, as soon as we let go we fall down and don't want to get back up.

I believe accountability and having other people speak into our lives is very important. Unfortunately, too many Christians abuse accountability. An immature Christian thinks that other people are responsible to hold him up and keep him walking. He believes that if they don't, then it's their fault if he falls. He never learns to stand up and take responsibility for his own walk. He doesn't take responsibility for implementing the Word of God in his own life. It's time to get a hold of determination and say, *"I'm going to learn how to walk. I'm going to learn to continually find things in the Word of God and apply them in my life. I'm not going to have to have people hit me between the eyes for ten years with the same Scripture before I apply it to my own life."*

When you learn truth begin to walk in it, begin to live it, begin to do what you know is right. Spend some time in prayer right now committing to have that holy determination to walk. Work hard to apply the truth to your life and walk it out.

Memorize 3 John 3 right now. Write it on a card and take it with you all day. Meditate on walking in the truths you have learned.

DAY FIVE: MANY OF US WOULD STILL BE CRAWLING IF WE DID PHYSICALLY WHAT WE DO SPIRITUALLY.

One thing you notice about a child who is learning to walk is that he falls down a lot. He falls down and gets back up. After repeatedly falling and getting back up, he will get really frustrated if after a while he isn't better at walking. Too many Christians start learning to walk but then fall down and say, *"Forget it, I'll never learn to walk. Forget it, it's too hard. I can't really learn to do this."* Because they have no heart, they have no determination. As a child you had determination. You continued to pull yourself up and take another step and another step.

If many of us did physically when we were babies what we have done spiritually, we would have never learned to walk. We would still be crawling right now. But you were determined. No matter how many times you fell, you continued to get up. If you look at most adults they spend much more time walking than they do sitting or crawling, but when they first began to walk, they had never taken a step in their life. Maybe you feel like that. Maybe you have never taken a step spiritually in your life. You have never let go and walked on your own, so you wonder how it could ever be possible.

The Bible says, *Though a righteous man falls seven times, he rises again* (Proverbs 24:16). Continue with this determination: Apply the Word of God in your life and live this Christian life. I know you can do it. God says you can do it. Refuse to stay sitting down. The devil wants to intimidate you to make you think that you're always going to be a failure, that you're never going to be able to walk, that you're never going to be able to stand by yourself. He wants you to think that you are never going to be able to live this Christian life. If he can intimidate you enough and cause you to live in fear, then you'll sit down and you won't move. Then you'll never be effective in God's Kingdom. We see too many Christians just sitting in church, sitting at home, laying in bed, crawling around. They're not applying what they have learned. We are not supposed to be like the world; we're supposed to show the world the way. The world doesn't see enough Christians walking it out. But God is beginning to do this great thing among young people all across the land. The world wants somebody to show them how to walk it out. They want somebody to look at to be able to say, "That's what a mature Christian looks like. That's what a person looks like who really walks out this Christian life."

I want you to begin to chew on Proverbs 24:16 today: *Though a righteous man falls seven times, he rises again.* Build your foundation; build your platform. Be determined that you are going to be one of those who always gets back up.

Take a few minutes now to write out your prayer committing to keep getting up to walk out your Christian life.

_____

_____

_____

_____

_____

_____

_____

_____

_____

DAY SIX: WALKING IN OBEDIENCE IS THE SIGN OF A MATURE CHRISTIAN.

2 John 6: *And this is love: that we walk in obedience to his commands. As you have heard from the beginning, his command is that you walk in love.* Please rewrite this in your own words now.

_____

_____

_____

_____

_____

_____

_____

_____

Standing up and learning how to walk is simply learning to walk in obedience, obeying what you know is right . Obey what you know the Lord has convicted you of and you walk in obedience; it's amazing!

I have three children, and I have seen each of them go through the amazing process of learning how to walk. They seem like such babies as they crawl and pull themselves up. They roll around on the ground, almost as if they just came out of the womb. Then they stand a little bit and fall, stand a little bit and fall, but they still look like babies. Then they learn to walk a little bit while I am holding them, but they still seem like babies. Then that day comes when they take that first step by themselves, and within a week, they're walking around the entire house unassisted. Something happens, all of a sudden they don't look like babies anymore. Their whole countenance changes. Their whole sense of confidence changes, and the entire world becomes available to them. Mobility is no longer an issue to them. They can go where they want, when they want, without having to have a parent carry them.

When you learn to walk in obedience, the same thing will happen to you. A whole new world of possibilities will be open to you. You will have a whole new strength, a whole new realm of what God can do through you because He can trust you now. As God sees that you are serious about applying His Word and walking in obedience, He knows that He can trust you in other areas. He can trust you to be a leader because He knows that as other people look to you they're going to see somebody who's walking in obedience. You're going to be able to do things like go on mission trips and take over your school with the Gospel of Jesus. You'll get to do things that other people only hope to do while everybody else is crawling around, crying and squealing like babies. While others are hanging on like leeches, depending on other people to help them walk and stand, you will be there blazing a trail for others to follow.

Walking is a sign of a maturing child. When he starts walking, you know he's growing up. And walking in obedience is a sign of a mature Christian. As a mature Christian, when God begins to convict your heart, you need to do everything you can to change that part of your life. You pull yourself up. You walk in obedience in that area of your life. You're not obeying just because your mama screamed at you or because your youth pastor preached to you about it a thousand times. You change your life because you want to be obedient to the Word of God and to the Holy Spirit.

It's time for this world to see a new standard of young Christians who can walk in faith. They need to see a generation that walks in obedience, that walks in the light, that walks in truth. You need to be one of those. Take 2 John 6 and chew on it all day long. Learn how to walk today.

DAY SEVEN: YOU MUST LEARN TO STAND AND WALK.

I want you to review what you have learned this week. Review all the Scriptures that you have been chewing on. Take them all with you today and meditate on them all day long. What are some areas in your life that you know God has been wanting you to get up and walk in but you have been crawling in for too long? Write them here.

_____

_____

_____

_____

_____

_____

_____

_____

_____

_____

Now commit to the Lord that you're going to stand up and walk in these areas. Commit to the Lord that you're going to have a heart of determination no matter what. You're going to pull yourself up again and again and again. Commit to find Scriptures, to cram them down your throat, to cram them into your heart. Commit that you'll not be an air-headed mindless leech of a Christian for the rest of your life, but you'll plant your feet on the solid rock of Jesus. Commit to the Lord your determination to walk in obedience all the days of your life.

ACTION POINTS

What am I going to do in response to what I learned this week?

_____

_____

_____

_____

_____

_____

_____

_____

_____

_____

_____

_____

_____

_____

_____

_____

....

WHAT'S COMING OUT OF YOUR MOUTH?

DAY ONE: OUR WORDS SHOULD SHOW THAT WE HAVE SUBSTANCE.

As a baby gets older she learns how to articulate syllables and, ultimately, how to talk. But it's a painfully slow process. The parent can tell the maturity level of the child, especially when someone else comes over to the house and says, *"Wow, your baby sure is talking a lot."* Usually she begins to talk, and you don't realize how many words she knows.

She starts with the cooing and all the baby talk, and many parents talk to their child in baby talk. We all think it's cute, and it's adorable to watch her try to mimic her mom and dad and say things that sound like words. We laugh at the way she enunciates or pronounces certain words like saying, *"wa wa"* for water and so forth. If she says her *"s"* with a *"th,"* we think it's cute for a while. But there comes a point when the child is expected to speak correctly. If she still says *"wa wa"* when she's six years old nobody thinks it's cute. If she is still lisping when she's twelve years old everybody knows there is a speech impediment. Many Christians have never really overcome their speech impediments. They are still talking like babies, like baby Christians. They show that they are not very deep in the Lord by the way they talk.

So much of our talk about God is "Christian-eze." You know, all the Christian slang we've always heard but have never really given much thought to. We say, *"God is awesome. God is cool. Let's be sold out to Him."* We say things mindlessly without really thinking about what we're saying. We'll shout it at a concert or at a youth camp, but our talk of the things of God never gets much deeper than that. That's why it is so hard for many of us to witness and share our faith. All we have is a surfacey faith, so that's all we'll know to talk about. If our faith never gets very deep, we can't articulate anything deep. If we're not very deep, it's hard for us to convince somebody that Jesus is alive inside of us and that it's something they really need.

In some churches you'll hear people say over and over again things like, *"Praise the Lord, Glory to God, Hallelujah, Amen."* These words are Christian-eze—mindless, spiritual words that come flowing out of the mouth but have no substance to them. Somebody might think, *"Well, I'd say something deep, if I knew something deep to say."* That's the whole point. If you want to say something deep, you need to be deep. Dive into the Word of God to get deep so you've got something deep to say. When God begins to do deep things in you and you're working through issues, temptations, and problems that you've been going through, and you get victory and learn how to stand, then you'll have something deep to say.

You could say that an athlete works really hard. But that athlete could tell you how many sit-ups and how much running, sweating, working out he does. He could tell you exactly what he did to get to that level of fitness. In the same way, people who are not strong Christians look at the Christian walk and say, *"All you have to do is this, all you have to do is that. Oh, just be excited about God. Just be committed to Him, and you'll be strong."* Their air-headed statements show that they have never really done the workout.

Colossians 4:6 say, *Let your conversation be always full of grace, seasoned with salt, so that you may know how to answer everyone.*

Write this verse in your own words.

_____

_____

_____

_____

_____

_____

_____

The things that we say should constantly give off a taste that shows we have substance to our life. Begin to meditate on Colossians 4:6 today and ask the Lord, *"Lord, what kind of salt can I give off today? What can I say today that might strike people in their hearts or minds to let them just get a glimpse that You are real in my life."*

DAY TWO: ONE SIGN OF SPIRITUAL IMMATURITY AND INSECURITY IS THE OVERUSE OF SPIRITUAL WORDS.

One of the things small children are famous for is blurting out words at inappropriate times. They might scream real loud or say a funny word in the middle of a church service. Everybody chuckles and realizes that it is just a child saying something out of order because she is not old enough to know any better. She'll be loud, obnoxious, and repetitive, but it's all acceptable because she's just a child.

We are talking this week about what comes out of your mouth and how what you say reflects what is going on in your life and your maturity as a Christian. Many Christians who have been around church for a long time are just like little children. They are loud and obnoxious. They say things that don't make any sense. They repeat themselves. They say things that are overly spiritual when they think they will be noticed. They might shout *"Hallelujah"* in church real loud, and then look around to see if anybody noticed how spiritual they look. At first their funny statements or jokes might be interesting or clever, but after a while it's usually a demonstration that they just want to be noticed or have attention drawn to themselves. It's the same way a child becomes obnoxious and shows her immaturity. It's a sign of insecurity.

Many Christians use overly spiritual words on a regular basis to make it look like they're spiritual on the outside, when really they feel very shallow inside. You can see that one sign of spiritual immaturity and insecurity is the overuse of "spiritual words" to make it look like we're something we're not. Do you always have to be the first one with a *Hallelujah*? We've all been around Christians who have said embarrassing things about the Lord or just things that embarrass us as Christians. A Christian may say something that makes us all look bad, or he may just say things at inappropriate times.

Sometimes in the middle of a youth service or prayer somebody sneezes, says something funny, or makes some kind of a rude gesture. Ephesians 5:4 says, *Nor should there be obscenity, foolish talk or coarse joking, which are out of place, but rather thanksgiving.* Please, write in your own words what this verse means.

_____

_____

_____

_____

This verse is saying that we need to be mature believers. We need to be mature in what we say. Don't just say silly little coy things to try to be cute. We don't need to try to be cute, and we don't need to try to get other people's attention. If we know who we are in Christ, if we know that God made us awesome and incredible people, that we are new believers with a new heart, then we don't have to feel insecure. We don't have to feel less than par. We don't have to try to live up to anybody else's standards; we just do what the Bible says. We don't need to try to look like something on the outside that we're not on the inside. We don't need to get our security by having other people laugh at our jokes. Just be who you are: a confident Christian. With this confidence, you don't always have to have a joke, be the funny man, or say something silly to get other people's attention.

I want you to take a few minutes this morning to evaluate your own talking, both what you say and how you say it. What level of maturity would people say you have based on what you say and how you talk? What could you change today about what you say and how you say it to show that you are maturing as a young believer. Write these things down.

_____

_____

_____

_____

Now pray about these areas today. Demonstrate that you are growing by the way you talk.

DAY THREE: DON'T BE THE KIND OF PERSON WHO SPREADS POISON.

An important area we need to deal with in the way we talk as we mature in Christ is how we talk about others. In the world we live it is so easy and even normal to cut other people down, talk bad about them, make fun of them, stab them in the back, and make ourselves look better than others—whether it's a leader, a friend, or our parents. This world is constantly teaching us to do whatever we can to make other people look bad and to make ourselves look good. The Bible talks very clearly about this, *Do not judge, or you too will be judged* (Matthew 7:1). It also talks about gossiping. Titus 3:2 says, *to slander no one, to be peaceable and considerate, and to show true humility toward all men.*

Speaking like a mature believer means holding our tongue while other people let their tongues fly. When others are cutting people down, we don't jump in the middle of it. We don't agree with them. When we see something that is bad about somebody else we don't state the obvious. If other people want to notice it, they can. Even if you find out something that is bad about somebody else that is true, you don't want to be one of those people who spread bad reports.

You have to ask yourself this question: What do you want emanating from your life? Do you want joy and peace? Do you want a godly aura of Christian character? Or do you want poison, venom, negativity, and a bad attitude emanating from your life. What you sow is what you reap. If you are the kind of person who spreads poison, then people will say bad things about you as well and your poison will come back on you.

In addition, it's a sign of immaturity. As soon as children are able to talk, they start saying they want their way. If something goes wrong they blame somebody else, either a brother or a sister. They have no restraints. They have no control over their lips. They say whatever and slam whoever comes to mind or is target for making fun of.

Think about it. Are there people you have talked about in a negative way in the last week or two? I'm constantly having to hold my tongue because as a leader I find out all kinds of things about other people. I am constantly rebuking myself when something slips out of my mouth that I know didn't really lift up somebody else. That attitude should be the standard. Even if you know something negative and it's true, are you lifting other people up when you talk about it? Are you passing along gossip. Even if it is true gossip, it still is not a mature, godly thing to do.

Write down the names of anybody you have talked about this week.

_____

_____

_____

_____

_____

_____

_____

Now I want you to ask God to forgive you and start praying for these people. Think of some positive things you can say about each one of those people, and try to repair some of the damage you have done to their reputations.

Take a few minutes to meditate on Matthew 7:1 and Titus 3:2. Write them out on cards and carry them with you. Whenever you are tempted to talk about someone, pull these cards out and read them again.

DAY FOUR: WHOLESOME TALK IS A SIGN OF CHRISTIAN MATURITY.

Ephesians 4:29: *Do not let any unwholesome talk come out of your mouths, but only what is helpful for building others up according to their needs, that it may benefit those who listen.* Please write this Scripture out in your own words.

_____

_____

_____

_____

_____

_____

_____

I think about the concept of *unwholesome talk*. The Bible says let no unwholesome talk come from your mouth. "Unwholesome" can sure include a lot of different areas. It can mean cussing or vulgar jokes. In our society it is hard for us to distinguish between wholesome and unwholesome. What we hear on TV and radio and in music and movies seems so bad. And it is hard to distinguish whether what you're talking about is unwholesome or not. The standard we need to use is the Bible, the kinds of things Jesus and the apostle Paul talked about. Is it true, is it lovely, is it worthy of praise, is it uplifting (Philippians 4:8)? Or is it a joke that you would be embarrassed to say in front of Jesus? If so, then why would you say it to one of your friends? Is the topic of a conversation you were having with one of your friends one that you would be embarrassed to have broadcast over a loudspeaker at your church? Then, why would you even talk about it?

If there's anything that you're saying that you would be embarrassed about anybody else knowing—your parents or your pastor—then why would you say it at all? Wholesome talk is a sign of maturity.

It's a sign that you have grown past the games that children play of saying little dirty or off-colored things that are just a little bit wrong and then laughing about it. When their parents say, *"What are you talking about?"* They say, *"Oh, nothing, nothing, nothing."* Maturity is wanting to talk about things that are wholesome and right because it's the right thing to do, not out of fear that your conversation may be broadcast on a PA system for your whole church to hear.

Take four minutes now and meditate on Ephesians 4:29. Chew on it, and chew on it, and chew on it. Take it with you all day long. Write it down on a card so that anytime you're tempted to say something unwholesome, you can pull this Scripture out and say it instead. This way you can get your talking in line with what a mature believer would say.

DAY FIVE: YOUR TONGUE CONTROLS YOUR DESTINY.

James 3:5-6: *Likewise the tongue is a small part of the body, but it makes great boasts. Consider what a great forest is set on fire by a small spark. The tongue also is a fire, a world of evil among the parts of the body. It corrupts the whole person, sets the whole course of his life on fire, and is itself set on fire by hell.*

Take a few minutes now to meditate on these verses.

Here the Bible is telling us that the direction of our whole life is set by our tongue. If you say positive things then you plant a positive seed and positive stuff is going to come your way. Your tongue could be a fire and ruin people's lives or reputation, or it could be a blessing to people. You can't just say, *"Oh, I felt like talking about this,"* or *"No, I didn't feel like talking about this."* Your tongue controls your destiny, it controls the direction of your whole life.

People say, *"Well, I just can't help it if I have a bad attitude or if I'm having a bad day."* Well, the Bible says you can help it, because the way you talk can change your attitude. You say positive things, you say Scriptural things, and you set the pace for a Scriptural day. When you say negative things, then you set a curse for your day. The Bible says your tongue is a small thing, like the rudder of a ship.

Many of us can barely control our tongue in church on Sunday, much less the rest of our week. We wonder why so much of our life is falling apart, why so many bad things are happening to us. Well, one thing you need to check is your tongue. There are some people you just love to be around because they say things to inspire, encourage, lift, and exhort you. You can't wait to be around them because you feel like you can do anything because of what they say to you. That's the kind of person you need to seek to be today. That's a mature believer, not looking for people to compliment you, but looking for people you can compliment.

Maybe you never realized how much power your tongue has in your life and the lives of those around you. You can walk into a classroom and totally set the pace for the day in a positive way, or you can set the pace for the day in a negative way. You can do the same thing with your youth group and with your family. It's your tongue, you can choose how you are going to use it. A mature believer says, *"You know what, I'm going to use my tongue to point people toward God, toward hope, toward Jesus."*

Write down three things you can say in different situations you might face today. Keep in mind that your goal is to find words that will point people toward Jesus and toward a great experience in their day.

_____

_____

_____

_____

_____

_____

_____

Now, pray over these words as you prepare to say them. You're not going to say these words on accident; you're going to prepare and plan to use your tongue in the right way. In the same way a captain on a ship has to plan which way he's going to steer that rudder, you have to plan today how you are going to steer the rudder of your tongue to use it as a blessing.

DAY SIX: IF YOU CAN CONTROL YOUR TONGUE, YOU CAN CONTROL ANYTHING.

James 3:8: *But no man can tame the tongue. It is a restless evil, full of deadly poison.*

The Bible talks about "taming the tongue." We said yesterday that if you can control your tongue you can control anything and that taming your tongue is a sign of a mature believer. People say, *"Well, I just can't help it."* The fact is, you can help it. You can tame your tongue. *"I can do everything through him who gives me strength"* (Philippians 4:13). Your tongue is not your boss. You are the boss of your tongue.

I want to encourage you in your growth as a mature believer every day in your quiet times to purpose in your heart the kind of things you're going to say. Just like yesterday you planned words that you can use in every situation, how you're going to start a day, how you're going to start a conversation, how you're going to treat people. Are you going to say, *"God bless you,"* or are you going to say, *"Adios"*? Are you going to say something that lifts them as you leave? Let's say somebody starts to share gossip with you. Decide in advance how you will treat that gossip no matter who it is about. Are you going to say, *"Hey, I don't want to hear that,"* or are you going to repeat it to somebody else? That is what taming your tongue is. It's planning in advance what you're going to say and how you're going to respond so you don't accidentally get yourself in trouble or let your tongue run out of control.

Begin to make this a regular part of your quiet time. As you are praying through your day say, *"God, give me the right words to say in these situations I'll face today. Make me a man or woman who exudes maturity in a solid relationship with Christ because of the kinds of things that are coming out my mouth today. Let them not be just arrogant, air-headed, or obnoxious, but let them be something that goes deep into the heart of the people who are listening. Let me use words that will point their attention toward you, in Jesus name, Amen."*

Write Proverbs 18:21 on an index card. *The tongue has the power of life and death, and those who love it will eat its fruit.* Take it out often today and meditate on it. Will you bring life or death to others today?

DAY SEVEN: WHAT'S COMING OUT OF YOUR MOUTH?

We have been talking all week about how you use your tongue, and how your use of it reflects your maturity level in Christ. I Peter 3:10 says, *Whoever would love life and see good days must keep his tongue from evil and his lips from deceitful speech.*

Write your own interpretation of this Scripture.

_____

_____

_____

_____

_____

_____

_____

_____

_____

The whole point of our week is that if you want a full life, if you want a great life, then you have to control your tongue. If you keep your tongue from evil you'll have a life that is worth living, and people will love being around you. There will be joy and hope on your lips; you'll be an encouragement. Keeping evil from our lips isn't something that will happen by accident; it doesn't come naturally just because we're believers. You have to purpose in your heart to take control of your tongue. If you want the fullness and richness of all the joy in life that God has promised, it starts with what you say.

Keeping your tongue from evil when most people's tongues are bent on evil is a sure mark that you are not just an average "Joe" Christian, that you're not just an average "Joe" person. You don't accidentally say what you say. You purpose in your heart what you are going to say, just like Jesus did.

At one point Jesus said, *For I did not speak of my own accord, but the Father who sent me commanded me what to say and how to say it* (John 12:49). Let this be your testimony. There was a time in my life when I was loud and obnoxious, and I talked too much. I had to purpose in my heart that I was going to shut my mouth and learn to listen to people. Then I had to decide to use my tongue carefully in conversations and say only what I knew would bring glory to God in public.

Take a few minutes and review each of the Scriptures this week. Review the Scriptures you have memorized and the notes that you have made. Take a few minutes and pray over your lips and your tongue. Purpose in your heart from this point on that you are going to commit your lips and your tongue to the Lord. Acknowledge that these are His lips and this is His tongue, and they will only be used to glorify Him all your days. By this you will show the world another glimpse of what a mature believer looks like.

ACTION POINTS

What am I going to do in response to what I learned this week?

_____

_____

_____

_____

_____

_____

_____

_____

_____

_____

··

GROWING UP IN THE WAY WE THINK

DAY ONE: WISDOM COMES FROM DOING THINGS GOD'S WAY.

Luke 2:52: *Jesus grew in wisdom and stature and favor with God and man.* Write out in your own words what you think this verse means.

_____

_____

_____

_____

_____

_____

_____

_____

Take as much time as you need right now to memorize this verse.

Isn't it amazing that Jesus was the Son of God, yet He still had to grow in wisdom? He had to grow up in the way He thought about things. The Greek word for "to grow" means to drive forward, to advance, to increase, to proceed. If we want to become mature believers, we have to start getting away from having others think for us. There are too many people who are simply air-head Christians, mindless in their Christianity. They don't think about what they're doing or how to grow. They just go to church and then go home.

Think about this: Jesus didn't do anything by accident. He thought through everything He was going to do, and then He did it with wisdom. There needs to be part of our mind and heart that is constantly seeking to grow. If we are going to seek to be like Jesus, we have to do the things He's doing. That's growing in wisdom. We should always be increasing in our wisdom. You don't have to be old to be wise. Wisdom comes from doing things God's way. It's knowing the way God would want something done, and doing it appropriately, even if it seems illogical or unimportant to the world. Wisdom is going against the way we would naturally think and the way we would naturally do things, and saying, *"God, I want to find out the way you think about this situation so I can do it accordingly."* I've talked to some young people who by their words demonstrate they have an incredible amount of wisdom. It doesn't matter how old you are. What matters is your eagerness to dive in, get wisdom, and apply it to the way you think and live.

List some areas here that you wish you had more wisdom in, areas where you could have avoided some really big mistakes if you had applied that wisdom:

_____

_____

_____

_____

_____

Now make a decision that even though you're young, you're going to be one of the people who determines to drive forward, to increase, to advance in the wisdom that you are beginning to walk in so you don't keep making the same mistakes.

DAY TWO: MATURE CHRISTIANS HAVE LEARNED TO THINK FOR THEMSELVES.

We maturing in the way we think when we learn to think for ourselves. Too many people let everybody else do their thinking for them. They are constantly asking questions that prove they don't think for themselves. They ask their youth pastor questions like, *"Where should I put this piece of garbage?"* Where do you think you should put it? It's a piece of garbage—put it in the trash. Or they ask their parent a question that they've asked a hundred times before. Too many people just live like robots. They do whatever they're programmed to do. They keep asking for more direction, and they let someone else tell them what to do rather than thinking for themselves. God is wanting us to grow up and learn how to think for ourselves.

Young children, before they're able to think for themselves, need a lot of direction. The parents must think for them at first. Parents tell their child not to touch the stove. The child doesn't know that it's going to burn her because she has never felt the hot stove before. The parents can't let the child get near enough to the stove to learn how hot it is. A child can't understand the intensity of the heat, so the parents tell him not to touch. The child doesn't know that a car is going to run over him or hit him, so the parents tell him not to run into the middle of the road. They tell the child to hold their hands when he's walking in or near the street. After a time, there comes a point when the parents expect their children to learn how to think for themselves. The parents explain the rules several times until the child learns not to touch the hot stove or run into the street. The child must learn that he has to follow the rules even when the parents aren't there making him obey. They obey not because they are forced, but because they've learned to think for themselves.

The story of the Prodigal Son (Luke 15:11-32) is a great example of learning the hard way to think for yourself. The son wanted to do his own thing, but he did it without thinking about the consequences. Finally, he loses all of the money his dad gave him, and he's had to get a job feeding the pigs. Then, *he came to his senses.* He began to think for himself. He thought, *"Wait a minute, what am I doing? This is so illogical. This doesn't make any sense. I'm going to go back and do the right thing."* Instead of mindlessly doing what he was doing and wondering why all these bad things were happening to him, he woke up. He said, *"Even if I have to work as a slave at my Dad's house, it's better than staying here and starving."*

Instead of being like a child, just letting somebody else think for you, you must learn to ask why. Don't just do what you do; ask, *"Why am I doing what I'm doing?"* If your parents or your leaders ask you to do something, don't just do it mindlessly. Ask why in your own mind, *"Why does he want me to do this?"* And think through some of your own answers. Or ask them why, but do it in a respectful way. Don't do it like a little child who whines, *"WHY?"* when his parents ask him to do something. Seek to really understand why. If you seek to understand why, you'll gain wisdom so the next time you can draw the right conclusions yourself.

List some areas where you feel like you need to "come to your senses." List things you've been doing mindlessly without understand why you've been doing them. Just like the Prodigal Son, you need to say, *"Stop, wait a minute. Why am I doing this? I need to do it the right way."* Please write these areas out here:

_____

_____

_____

_____

_____

Commit these areas to God right now, and say, *"Lord, I'm going to come to my senses. I'm going to think about what I'm doing. I'm going to ask why when I do things the wrong way. How can I do it the right way?"* Practice thinking about what you do today. Ask yourself, *"Why am I doing this?"* and gain wisdom from what you do.

DAY THREE: THE LORD DESIRES US TO HAVE CONTROL OVER WHAT WE THINK.

We've probably all experienced days like this. Either we hung around the wrong crowd, or we didn't have a very good quiet time that day, but we end up doing something that's total, in-your-face sin. Something we know is stupid and wrong. When someone asks us, *"Hey, why did you do that?"* when we really stop to think about it, our only response is, *"I just wasn't thinking."* I don't know how many teenagers I have heard say, *"I just wasn't thinking. When I went to that party and took a drink, why wasn't I thinking? When I got messed up in the back seat of a car with that guy or that girl, I just wasn't thinking. When I cheated on that test, when I lied to my parents."* The list goes on and on. *"I just wasn't thinking."*

That's the problem. Too many Christians go to church their whole life, but they're not really thinking. Their life looks so much like a non-Christian's because they're not thinking about what they are doing. One of the biggest areas of control that the Lord wants us to have in our life is control over what we think. With our heart, we give our life to the Lord, but then we never let that penetrate our mind. If you're not thinking, you're going to do whatever your natural flesh wants to do that is sin. You'll say or do something and then wonder, *"Why did I do that? Am I not really saved?"* Yes, you are really saved. You've given your heart to God, but you need to let the commitment in your heart begin to change the way you think.

In Romans 12:1-2 the Bible says, *Therefore, I urge you, brothers, in view of God's mercy, to offer your bodies as living sacrifices, holy and pleasing to God—this is your spiritual act of worship. Do not conform any longer to the pattern of this world, but be transformed by the renewing of your mind. Then you will be able to test and approve what God's will is—his good, pleasing and perfect will.* The way you transform how you live is by renewing your mind and learning to think differently. You can't let your mind be the devil's playground anymore, just thinking whatever thoughts come to your mind. It's time to learn to take control and say, *"You know what, I'm going to renew my mind. I'm going to think new things, the things of the Word of God. I'm going to think the way God wants me to think."*

Too often we use the excuse, *"I just wasn't thinking."* It's a valid excuse. *"Well, it's really not my fault, not really my sin. I just wasn't thinking. I wasn't in my right mind; I wasn't doing it."* But God wants us to begin to renew our minds so that we are in our right mind. He wants us to control what we do by thinking about what we're doing and growing up in the way we think.

Take Romans 12:1-2 with you all day. Chew on it, meditate on it. Practice renewing your mind and thinking about everything you do before you do it today.

DAY FOUR: BY PUTTING GOD'S WORD IN YOUR MIND, YOU CHANGE THE WAY YOU THINK.

Proverbs 23:7: *For as he thinketh in his heart, so is he.* What do you think this means?

_____

_____

_____

_____

_____

Before you go on, take a few minutes to meditate on this verse.

Basically, the Bible says here whatever goes around in your heart and through your mind is really what you are made of. It reflects who you are. It's what you will do. The reason so many Christians have a hard time living a godly life is they never deal with what's going on in their thought life. There's no substance in their thoughts in terms of purposely thinking godly thoughts. As a result, they don't purposely do godly things. They wonder, *"What happened? Why did I do that."* That's why the Bible says that you must renew your mind. When you put God's Word in your mind, you change the way you think, which changes the way you are. *"As a man thinketh, so is he."*

In the same way, if you're thinking about garbage all the time, it's no surprise that you do garbage things. If you're thinking about blah things, then you'll live a blah Christian life. You're not forcing your brain to change the way you think and to think on the things that are in the Word of God. Your life will be ho-hum. It might even be pretty good. You may not be a bank robber or a murderer, but you'll never do anything great for God either. You'll blend into the woodwork and be another church goer. If you don't think as a mature Christian, you'll never act and live like a mature Christian.

That's why we have been emphasizing Scriptures throughout this book that you need to memorize and meditate on. If you're going to change the way you are, to become a mature Christian, first you must change the way you think.

DAY FIVE: AS MATURE CHRISTIANS OUR ATTITUDES DON'T RULE US, WE RULE THEM.

Let's talk about attitudes today. Attitudes are definitely part of the thought life. Sometimes we really intend to think the right way. Then suddenly something happens to us that we don't like. Somebody does something, our parents ask us to do something, somebody says something that offends us, and our attitude changes. Maybe we started the day with the intentions of really living godly and having godly actions towards other people, but something happened to our attitude and totally messed up our whole day.

Controlling your thoughts also means controlling your attitude. Don't let just anything set you off. Control yourself when those things come your way. Realize that the devil is going to use other people's comments and attitudes all day long to try to set you off and to get your thinking off. He knows that if he can get your thinking off, he can get your life off track.

Philippians 2:5-7 says, *Your attitude should be the same as that of Christ Jesus: Who, being in very nature God, did not consider equality with God something to be grasped, but made himself nothing, taking the very nature of a servant, being made in human likeness.* We need to have the same attitudes that Christ Jesus had. That is, we don't let anything take charge of us. Our attitudes don't rule us, we rule them.

I want you to pray about any bad attitudes you have had the last few days. What are the things that really push your button and make you have bad attitudes? Write those things down.

_____

_____

_____

_____

_____

_____

_____

Pray about these right now. Be determined as you launch into the day. *"In Jesus name, I refuse to let circumstances rule my attitude. I am committed to have the attitude of Christ Jesus."*

Write Philippians 2:5 on a card right now. Memorize it and meditate on it all day today. When something happens and you're tempted to have a bad attitude, pull out this verse and meditate on it. Think about how Jesus acted when people messed with Him and tried to get Him off track.

DAY SIX: TO HAVE THE PEACE OF GOD, YOU NEED TO DELIBERATELY PLANT GOD'S THOUGHTS IN YOUR MIND.

Philippians 4:8-9: *Finally, brothers, whatever is true, whatever is noble, whatever is right, whatever is pure, whatever is lovely, whatever is admirable—if anything is excellent or praiseworthy—think about such things. Whatever you have learned or received or heard from me, or seen in me—put it into practice. And the God of peace will be with you.* The Bible also says in Colossians 3:2, *Set your mind on things above, not on earthly things.* Before you go on, write out what you think these verses are telling you.

_____

_____

_____

_____

_____

_____

The Bible is telling us in these passages that we have to choose what we put our mind on. The good news is that our mind does not rule us and tell us what to do. A mature believer tells his mind what to think. Some people say, *"Well, I just can't help it. I just think bad thoughts."* The Bible says that the good news is not only that you can control your thoughts, but you can choose what you're going to set your mind on. The devil doesn't choose, God doesn't choose, you choose. God knows that your life will be changed if you change the way you think. He says whatever is good, whatever is awesome, whatever is worthy of honor and lifting up, those are the things we need to tell our minds to think on.

People act like they can't understand. *"Well, I prayed today. I had quiet times and I went to church this week. Why don't I have any peace? Why is my life so confused? Why is everything in a mess?"* The Bible says if you want peace, you need to think on these things. You don't just get peace by praying for peace. You don't get it by hoping for it, you don't get confusion out of your life just by saying you don't want confusion. You have to do the right thing. The right thing to do is to deliberately plant God's thoughts in your mind.

Take as much time as you need right now to memorize Philippians 4:8-9. Write it on an index card so you can review it all day and check your thoughts against it.

DAY SEVEN: WE NEED TO GROW UP IN THE WAY WE THINK.

We've been learning this week how to grow in wisdom. How do you continue to get wisdom? Proverbs 2:1-5 talks about this. Please read these verses now. What does it say you must do if you want wisdom?

_____

_____

_____

_____

_____

_____

_____

You can't just hope for it, you can't just ask for it. You have to long for it with all your heart. You have to want to grow in wisdom more than anything else. When King Solomon had a choice to ask for anything in the world, he said, *"Lord, give me wisdom."* And because he chose to ask for noble things, God gave him everything else that he didn't ask for, too. The same is true with you—if you get wisdom and begin to think in accordance with God's Word in a wise way, you'll get all the blessings and more than you can possibly imagine.

Obviously, if you've made it this far in the book you're a no-nonsense Christian. You want to make a difference. You want to do something with your life that counts. The important thing is to grow deep in the things of God so that as you begin to do great things, you have deep roots on the inside to match what you're doing on the outside. So many people want to do great things even though they aren't very deep on the inside. You have to grow deep in the Word of God, train your thoughts to think the thoughts of God, and pursue wisdom with everything in you.

I want you to take the time right now to memorize Proverbs 2:1-5. Write them down on a card, and take them with you. Make them your heart, your desire, your passion. Transform the way you think by cramming the Bible in your brain and seeking wisdom with all your heart. I want to encourage you today to think through all the Scriptures you used this week so you can leave this week with this holy determination. Decide that this is the way you're going to be. You are going to grow up as a mature believer. Begin to think the thoughts of God. Passionately pursue wisdom, not just this week but all of your life. Cry out for it. Call out for it. Yearn for it. Dive into the Bible and apply it to your mind. Refuse to be an immature Christian all your life. Be determined to grow up in the way you think.

ACTION POINTS

What am I going to do in response to what I learned this week?

_____

_____

_____

_____

_____

_____

_____

_____

_____

_____

_____

_____

_____

....

BECOME RESPONSIBLE FOR YOURSELF

DAY ONE: WHEN YOU TAKE RESPONSIBILITY FOR YOUR ACTIONS AND DO THE RIGHT THING, OTHERS WILL TAKE PLEASURE IN YOU.

From the time a baby is born, she basically needs to be waited on hand and foot. She needs to be fed, have her nose wiped, and have her bottom wiped. She needs to have everything done for her if she's to have any kind of sustenance. What happens after a while, though, is the baby begins to learn to do those things on her own. As we've already studied, she learns to eat. At first she's not very good at it and she's not very neat, but she does learn to eat. Parents have to dress the child until she gets to be three, four, or five years old, and then she starts learning to put on her own pants, shoes, and shirt. By the time she's seven or eight she is picking out her own clothes, and her parents are expecting her to know how to match. Basically she's taking responsibility for dressing and feeding herself. She can't walk around in her underwear all day because nobody took the time to get her dressed. That's ludicrous. She knows, the family knows, everyone knows that she is responsible for getting herself dressed. Yet so many Christians come to church their whole life who have never been responsible for their own spiritual growth, for getting themselves dressed. They've never been responsible for their own actions.

We want to read again this morning and this week a verse from last week. Luke 2:52 says, *And Jesus grew in wisdom and stature and favor with God and man.* Let's talk about growing in favor with God and man. Take a few moments and write out what you think it means to grow in favor with God and man.

_____

_____

_____

_____

_____

_____

_____

_____

When you talk about favor you're talking about a reflection of your heart and your life. It's bringing pleasure to others, bringing joy to others, and doing what is acceptable to others. It gives you favor with other people, and it gives you favor with God. When you take responsibility for your actions and do the right thing, others will take pleasure in you. They take pleasure in what you did and how you acted without their even asking you to do it. This is a sign that you're beginning to be responsible. How pleasurable it is for a parent to see his young person thinking and doing the right thing without having to be told. It makes your parents and your leaders very happy when you do that. And remember, a happy parent is a generous parent. A happy parent is a kind parent. A happy parent is a parent who loves to give blessings. Many young people want the blessings from their parents—they want a car, a stereo, new clothes. But they forget the Scripture that God promised Abraham, *If you are obedient you will inherit the blessings of the earth.* If you're obedient and responsible, then you're growing in favor with your parents. Then, because they're more pleased, they're going to want to do more things for you even without your asking. We need to be on a quest to grow in our maturity as believers, to grow in favor, and to grow in responsibility. We need to do this so our parents and other leaders will be proud, but also so our God will be proud of what we're doing.

The first day a child comes out of the room dressed by himself, the first day he goes to the kitchen and gets breakfast for himself, he's taking responsibility for his own needs and actions. When your parents and God begin to see that kind of responsibility in you, you're going to find blessings begin to invade your life.

Review Luke 2:52 to make sure you still have it memorized. Meditate on it today, especially thinking about growing in favor with God and man.

DAY TWO: RESPONSIBILITY IS DOING THE RIGHT THING, EVEN WITHOUT BEING TOLD.

Colossians 3:22 says, *Slaves, obey your earthly masters in everything; and do it, not only when their eye is on you and to win their favor, but with sincerity of heart and reverence for the Lord.*

The verse is talking about how to be a faithful, responsible servant. It tells how to get favor with your boss if you're an employee, or with your parents in your home. Responsibility is doing the right thing even without being told. You know it's the right thing to get dressed so you do it, even though there's no one to tell you every day to get your clothes on. One way of showing maturity and demonstrating how well you handle responsibility is by doing what you're asked to do or what you know is right even no one's eye is on you. A mark of maturity as a Christian is being responsible for your actions and doing the right thing when no one else is around.

I want you to be honest with yourself and write down a few things that you have done when no one was looking that you knew weren't right. When you get to this point as you continue to grow in the Lord, you shouldn't be dealing with huge things like, *"I had sex when I thought I wouldn't get caught."* Hopefully you have already dealt with those kinds of actions, thoughts, and behaviors. We're talking about working in a restaurant and stealing a few fries when your boss was looking the other way. We're talking about watching something on TV that your parents told you not to watch, but watching it when they were not home. Write down things that you have done recently.

_____

_____

_____

_____

_____

Now repent and ask the Lord to forgive you. Make a commitment to do things the right way whether your boss, your parents, or anybody else is looking or not. You're on your way to maturity as a believer.

Memorize Colossians 3:22 right now. Say it out loud or to yourself whenever you're tempted to do wrong when no one is looking.

DAY THREE: A MATURE CHRISTIAN DOESN'T TRY TO HIDE A GUILTY CONSCIENCE.

Another mark of taking responsibility for yourself is what you do when you find that you've messed up and you've sinned. Whether it's a big sin or a small one, how long does it take for you to fess up to that? How long does it take for you to ask others' forgiveness when you hurt their feelings? How long does it take for you to ask God to forgive you when you've violated His law? 1 John 1:9 says, *If we confess our sins, he is faithful and just and will forgive us our sins and purify us from all unrighteousness.* He is faithful and just to forgive you. He's ready to forgive you, but He's looking for you to be responsible when you're wrong instead of pointing the finger to another person and saying, *"He made me do it."* Or, *"It was the peer pressure."* Proverbs 28:13 says, *He who conceals his sins does not prosper, but whoever confesses and renounces them finds mercy.* What happens to many Christians is they start sinning against the Lord and against other people, but they pretend they're not. They try to hide it from God and from other people, and they wonder why their lives get all messed up. They wonder why things don't go well for them, why there's no blessing on their lives, why their grades aren't very good, why things get taken away from them. They don't understand why they're affected in areas that don't have anything to do with the sin they committed. But the point is, when you sin you won't prosper. God's blessing won't be on your life. Proverbs 13:15 says that *the way of the transgressor is hard.*

The mark of a Christian's growing up is his quickness to come clean. He doesn't try to hide a guilty conscience. As soon as he feels a little bit of conviction from God, BOOM, he repents. If you hang onto the conviction from the Lord when He's trying to get rid of something from your life, pretty soon you can get a hard heart in that area, and you won't even think you've done anything wrong. A mature believer is someone who is quick to repent as soon as he feels conviction from God about how he treated another person or what he's done against God.

List here some ways you have sinned, things you have been slow to ask forgiveness for either from God or from others recently.

_____

_____

_____

_____

_____

_____

_____

Now make a commitment to be responsible for your own actions and quick to repent, whether it's a big or small thing, whether it's in front of God or in front of other people. The most important thing is to keep your heart pure and clean so that you can stay close to God. Then His favor will rest on you.

Take three minutes right now to memorize Proverbs 28:13.

DAY FOUR: YOU NEED TO TAKE RESPONSIBILITY FOR YOUR OWN SPIRITUAL GROWTH.

We are talking about being responsible. Think about that child again, eight or nine years old, who just doesn't want to dress himself. Are you making others responsible for dressing you every day? Another aspect of maturity is taking responsibility for your own growth. Do you make others responsible for your spiritual growth? In other words, will you fail to grow in the Lord if the youth pastor or the pastor doesn't have a great sermon? When you make statements like that you justify the fact that you're still a baby Christian. You're saying that you just can't help it. It's not your fault. That is as ridiculous as a ten-year-old child saying, *"It's my mama's fault I'm not dressed today,"* or a sixteen-year-old teenager saying, *"It's my dad's fault I'm not dressed today."* Are you taking responsibility for your own spiritual growth?

When you sin or mess up, do you point your finger at others? Or maybe you think it's not really a sin but it's a problem you have. You say something like, *"You see, because I have this problem, it's not really my fault. It's my problem's fault. If I didn't have this problem then I wouldn't have sinned."* Maybe you go to a counselor and then say, *"Well it's my counselor's fault that I have this problem. My counselor is not able to help me with this problem."* But this isn't just a problem; it is sin. A lot of people think that if a sin has been in their family for generations, it's not really sin but a genetic predisposition. *"It's not my problem that I steal, it's just that I'm prone to do it. I can't help it. It's not my fault I drink, it's in my genes."* And people cling to things like, *"Well, somebody in my family was an alcoholic so I really can't help it. It's just a problem that I have."* We candy coat sin by calling them problems, and we justify our way out without taking responsibility for them. We blame our past. *"Because of what happened to me I'm prone to get mad or get my feelings hurt or be shy. I can't help it if I cuss because of the way I was treated when I was younger."* When we blame others we sound self-righteous and self-justified, and we're simply not taking responsibility for our actions.

People like this never get anywhere in life. They never get anywhere in their spiritual life. They never grow. They never get anywhere in their physical life. They don't have a happy, wholesome family. They don't have a job where they continue to get promoted and blessed. People can't trust them with things. Bad things happen to them, and they're the first to point fingers at other people. They'll lose their job and say their boss is mean. They'll get a bad grade and say it's their teacher's fault. Somebody else will get promoted, and they'll say the boss just favored somebody else more. Whatever happens, it's never their own fault.

Is there something in your life that you're justifying because of your past or present hurts or because it's in your family? If there is, write it here.

_____

_____

_____

_____

We need to be the kind of people who show that we are spiritually mature by being the first to point the finger at ourselves. Before we look at anybody else we say, *"What could I have done differently? How could I have acted differently? How could I have prevented this situation?"* As an employer I like to hire those kind of people, and those are the people I like to promote. When the person takes responsibility, I can be assured that he will do whatever he can to help make it right.

Take a few minutes and review the Scriptures about being responsible for your own growth that we've looked at so far this week. Take the next five minutes to meditate and chew on them. Commit to take responsibility for your own growth and your own mistakes, as well as for your own victories.

DAY FIVE: GOD WANTS US TO BE RESPONSIBLE FOR OUR ACTIONS.

Let's take a moment today and talk about what it means to be responsible. The dictionary says that when you are responsible you are expected to account for something, that you are answerable to somebody. You are able to distinguish right from wrong and to think and act rationally. When most people think about teenage Christians, responsibility is not the first thing to pop into their mind. Most people think teenagers are easily swayed. They go one way, and then they go the other. They go back and forth and up and down, around and around and around. One minute they're excited about one thing, the next minute they're excited about another. But God wants us to be the kind of people who are willing to give an account for what we are doing. He wants us to be responsible for our actions. We are not to feel threatened or angry when others question our actions. If you did wrong and you're responsible, then confess. If you didn't do wrong then you can explain your actions so everybody can understand. You are accounting for what you've done. You are being responsible. Responsibility is clearly linked to thinking right. It's thinking rationally about what's right and what's wrong, and it's acting rationally as well. You have to have a clear mind.

One practical way to act responsibly is to do what it says in Proverbs 14:15: *A prudent man gives thought to his steps.* Write out your interpretation of what you think this means in teenage language.

_____

_____

_____

Now take a few minutes to memorize this verse.

I know it might sound like a bold new discovery for mankind or for all humanity because it looks like most people don't do this. However, a lot of people actually think before they do things—they give thought to their steps. What that means to you as a Christian is starting your day in your quiet times thinking through what you're going to do, where you're going to go, who you're going to be talking to. Give thought ahead of time because you're going to see some friends who always gossip. Think, what are you going to say? How are you going to handle yourself? If you know you are going to the store where there will be lots of non-Christians, what are you going to say? How are you going to act? Give thought to your steps. If you're going to be at ball practice, people will start cussing—what are you going to do? Don't wait until you are in the middle of everything. Think through what you are going to do before you get there so you can act responsibly according to what you have planned to do. Don't just wait until you're in the middle of a situation to see what happens. That's how most Christians act, and that's why most Christians have things happen to them. They come away surprised, *"I didn't really think I would do that. I don't know what happened."* And the cycle begins again of not taking responsibility for their actions. But as a mature believer, you're planning your whole day in prayer. You're thinking through everything. You're praying about and deciding how you're going to act, what Scriptures you're going to use, what attitudes you're going to have before you ever get there.

Now I want you to take a few moments and give thought to your steps for today. Where are you going? What are you going to do? Are you going to be in tempting situations? Think now how you're going to deal with that. Think now how you're going act when you're going to be with non-Christians. How will you handle the situation? Where you will be around other Christians, think now about how you will encourage them and lift them up, what you will say and do.

_____

_____

_____

_____

Pray over all of these steps that you want to take. Now go and live your life on purpose today. Give thought to your steps the way Jesus did. Never do anything by accident, but step out according to wisdom in all you do and say.

DAY SIX: WHEN YOU'RE RESPONSIBLE OVER LITTLE THINGS, GOD AND YOUR PARENTS CAN TRUST YOU WITH MORE.

Another reason to be a responsible Christian is that God will show you His favor. When God's favor is on you, you better watch out. He will blow you away with blessings. He will give you incredible opportunities. He will give you a shot at changing the world, changing the nation, making history. If He knows that you can be responsible with little, then He'll let you be responsible with much. In fact, Jesus told a parable about this. The climax of the parable is in Matthew 25:21, *You have been faithful with a few things; I will put you in charge of many things.* Read this parable right now. It's in Matthew 25:14-30. Take a few minutes now to memorize verse 21.

You may wonder why it's such a big deal to be responsible if you just lied or cheated. Who's going to ever know if you're not being responsible and confess what you've done? If you steal a pen from work, who's ever going to know? But God says it's all those little things that you act responsibly in that lets Him trust you with more. Not only can God trust you with more, but your boss and your parents can trust you with more, too. Then favor comes on your life, as well. You prove that you're responsible, and those people will trust you with more. You can look at Scriptural examples over and over again of God promoting people. For example, David's responsibility was sheep. He did a great job there, so God made him king.

Think right now of the things that you could be faithful and responsible with. Think of areas in your personal life where you've had sin or other struggles. Confess and be responsible for them. In school, take responsibility for your grades and for how you're doing in sports. Take responsibility in your job. Deal with issues between you and your parents, or you and your youth pastor. Think through areas where you can be faithful with a little now. You might have a little bit of responsibility, a little bit of freedom or opportunity given by your parents or your youth pastor. You think it's just a silly little thing, *"Oh, big deal, they let me go out with my friends."* But if you show you're faithful in that, it could mean a lot more favor and responsibility later. Write out some of those areas now that you can be faithful in the little things.

_____

_____

_____

_____

_____

_____

_____

_____

Now commit to be faithful to be responsible with these areas, to show that you are a thinking person and not just an air head bouncing through your day. Go show the world today what it looks like to be a responsible teenage Christian.

DAY SEVEN: YOU NEED TO BECOME RESPONSIBLE FOR YOURSELF.

The problem people have with being responsible is they think it means you can't have any more fun. The whole idea to being a teenager is just having fun. You think you don't have to be responsible yet. You don't have to work for a living right now. You can just have fun with your friends. You don't want to be responsible, you just want to have more fun. But some of the fun we want has to do with being responsible. So there you are being wild and crazy not having much responsibility at all, and you can't understand why your parents won't let you have your driver's license. You wonder why you can't have a bunch of friends over when your parents are gone. You wonder why you can't stay out later than eleven o'clock at night. Well, maybe you're so wild and crazy, so irresponsible, that they can't trust you with that stuff yet.

I want you to take a few minutes and review each of the six days this week, and write out three key things that you can see are marks of a responsible, mature Christian.

_____

_____

_____

_____

_____

_____

_____

_____

From all the things that you've learned this week, I want you to begin to apply these three. It may not make you more popular. It may not be what all your friends are doing, but it's time for you to go forth. It's time for you to start standing up and being the leader that this world needs you to be and that the Lord needs you to be. He's ready to do a great thing with this generation, and He needs people He can trust. He wants people who will be responsible in small things so He can give them responsibilities for big things. He needs people who will take responsibility for their own lives so He can give them responsibility to help disciple others and be responsible for their spiritual lives.

God is looking for people to pour out His favor on. You're pleasing Him when you take responsibility for your actions and thoughts, even when no one else is around. You're doing the right thing. You're growing and developing in maturity. You're not pointing the finger at everybody else. God looks at you and says, *"There's a young man, there's a young lady I can trust. I'm going to blow him (her) away with opportunities to make a difference and change this world."* Commit to it. You'll be glad you did. You will be blown away with God's blessings.

ACTION POINTS

What am I going to do in response to what I learned this week?

_____

_____

_____

_____

_____

_____

_____

_____

_____

MORE SIGNS OF MATURITY

DAY ONE: THOSE WHO ARE IMMATURE ARE TOSSED BACK AND FORTH; THOSE WHO ARE MATURE ARE STABLE.

We've been talking about growing up in the Lord. I hope that from these first eight weeks you can see specific ways that you have grown, begun to deepen your relationship with God, and shown signs of maturity in your walk with the Lord.

Take a moment as we begin this week to think through some of the things you have learned and what has changed about the way you live your life since you started this devotional book. What things are you doing now that are showing that you are developing maturity in your life?

_____

_____

_____

_____

_____

_____

I want to talk about specific signs the Bible says we'll see as we develop maturity. Ephesians 4:13-15, *Until we all reach unity in the faith and in the knowledge of the Son of God and become mature, attaining to the whole measure of the fullness of Christ. Then we will no longer be infants, tossed back and forth by the waves, and blown here and there by every wind of teaching and by the cunning and craftiness of men in their deceitful scheming. Instead, speaking the truth in love, we will in all things grow up into him who is the Head, that is, Christ.* Those who are immature are tossed back and forth, but those who are mature are stable. The immature get blown back and forth by a number of things. Sometimes they get blown by temptations. They barely start to get strong, then get out there with friends and around the same environment that they were involved with before. Their roots aren't very deep so they get blown over. Sometimes they are blown by different doctrines. Somebody will start preaching about some specific aspects of the Bible and the immature person starts thinking it is the most important thing and his life gets out of balance. A mature person is somebody who has studied the Word of God long enough to see through deceptions like that. He maintains wholeness and balance in his life no matter what. His theology is not freaked out and his roots are deep enough in the foundation of Jesus so he can be around the world and not get blown over.

If you find that you are easily swayed or easily falling, that is a sign that you are not mature enough and you to need get your roots down deep in that area. I want you to be the kind of person who has built up so much resilience that no matter what the world does against you, you can stand strong in your faith, no longer tossed around.

You've learned by now that the best way to get strong is to keep cramming God's Word down into your heart and in your mind. Spend five minutes now meditating on Ephesians 4:13-15. Write it on an index card so you can carry it with you all day today.

DAY TWO: A MATURE CHRISTIAN DIGS INTO THE WORD OF GOD TO UNDERSTAND THE WAYS AND HEART OF GOD.

Hebrews 5:14: *But solid food is for the mature, who by constant use have trained themselves to distinguish good from evil.* The Bible says something very interesting here. Somebody who is mature has the ability to distinguish between good and evil. That's an important point because a lot of people think its just natural—anyone can tell right from wrong. But it doesn't say right from wrong, it says good from evil.

In our society, so many wrong things are done that people don't think they are wrong anymore. So everything starts to look gray. Is it really right? Is it really wrong? Is it really good? Is it really evil? We even say things like, *"That's really bad,"* when we really mean *"That's really good."* We say something like, *"Oh, he's just a little goody-two-shoes,"* and it's a derogatory thing. We get such a skewed concept of what is right and wrong. I have even heard on television programs an unmarried woman saying to a man, *"Don't you know I've got morals. I don't sleep with more than one man at a time."* It's what the world calls moral or ethical, good. This is a virtuous person, even though she's not married. She only sleeps with one person at a time.

The Bible says that a mature believer digs into the Word of God and understands the ways and the heart of God so clearly that he can discern good from evil. Sometimes you won't even know why you feel something is evil. It's just in your spirit. You know it's just wrong and you shouldn't be doing it.

I have two little girls at home. Since they were very young, we have tried to teach them good versus evil. We don't watch regular TV channels anymore, but when we did, it was interesting to watch them flip through channels. They would watch for a few minutes and then come and tell us, *"We just changed the channel because we thought something was wrong with that show. Something wasn't right."*

Truth tastes good. When you're used to eating truth from the

Word of God and you taste something that is not truth—not good, right, and pure—you can taste that it is bad. The deeper you get in God, the more clearly you can see right versus wrong, and why good is good and evil is evil. It will be easier for you to see black and white when there is so much difference from the world perspective in what is right and wrong. If you can't see right from wrong then you will keep doing wrong things accidentally. You might think, *"Well, God doesn't hold me responsible for that."* But you still get yourself in trouble because if you're doing wrong things which are not righteous, you're going to reap foolishness and death and destruction in your own life. You can be bringing destruction in your own life and not even realize it because you're inadvertently doing evil. That's why you have to press in. You have to learn good from evil so the curse will be lifted off your life and you can walk in God's blessing in every part of your life.

Take Hebrews 5:14 right now and begin to meditate on it for the next four minutes. Then take it with you all day asking the Lord to give you a clear vision to be able to distinguish between wrong and right, between good and evil today.

DAY THREE: A MATURE CHRISTIAN IS FULLY ASSURED IN WHAT HE BELIEVES.

Colossians 4:12: *Epaphras, who is one of you and a servant of Christ Jesus, sends greetings. He is always wrestling in prayer for you, that you may stand firm in all the will of God, mature and fully assured.*

The Bible says here that somebody who is mature and growing up as a Christian is fully assured in what he believes. Think about the concept "fully assured." So many Christians go to church every week, but they are not fully assured. They prayed the prayer to give their life to Jesus, but if you ask them if they know where they would go if they died tonight, they would say, *"Well, I think I would go to heaven."* What do you mean you think? Do you really believe this Bible or not? Is it really true or not? They give mental assent or sort of believe it's the right way to go, but they are not fully assured. When Jesus died on the cross, He was fully assured that His blood would pay the price for people so that they could go to heaven. He wasn't thinking, *"Oh, maybe I should go, maybe I shouldn't. I'm not really sure if it is going to help anybody or not."* Jesus was fully assured. He was confident. He knew He was doing the right thing.

Christians who are mature are fully assured that they believe in the Creator God and that His Son was the only Son. They believe that He came to redeem all of mankind and that they are totally free from sin and the slavery to it. They won't feel the guilt of all the things they've done and then keep asking God to forgive them over and over again. No, they are fully assured. They are confident that they are forgiven. Understand, I am not saying that mature Christians are cocky or arrogant, but they are confident. They know their God. They know God is with them. They can get to a scary situation and have faith that God will protect them because they know what His Word says. They can pray for somebody who is sick and be fully assured that God is going to heal that person. They know what His Word says, that He loves to heal people. Jesus did it all the time.

Something happens when you are fully assured, a deep residing confidence sparkles in your eye knowing that God isn't just a Sunday thing, just a Wednesday thing. There is a conviction that will live inside of you knowing that you know God, knowing that your life is changed, knowing that you have met with the Most High.

This morning, I want you to take three minutes and meditate on this verse. Say it over and over and over again until you are almost sick of it. Now, I want you to begin to just spend time with the Lord this morning. Ask Him, *"Lord, help me to be fully assured. Help me to be fully convinced that what I believe is true. Help me to understand that the reality of my life has been totally changed from the inside out since You came to live in me."*

DAY FOUR: THE MATURE CHRISTIAN FINDS GREAT JOY IN PRAYER.

Probably one of the most profound signs of a mature believer can be found in what happens in his everyday prayer life. There are many people who just go into prayer. They pray whatever is on their emergency list, whatever is on their need list. They find themselves in deep prayer and intercession only when there is a crisis in their life. This is just part of an average ho-hum Christian life. But a mature believer is somebody who finds great joy in prayer. He finds himself escaping like Jesus did in Mark 1:35, *Very early in the morning, while it was still dark, Jesus got up, left the house and went off to a solitary place, where he prayed.* When no one else is looking he tries to sneak away to spend more time with God. He sits down in the middle of the day, maybe in-between classes, just to go and hang with God for a little while. He doesn't bring a bunch of lists in, but he prays over his list and he knows God will do it. But the most exciting part of prayer is just spending time with his Father getting to know Him better. A mature believer realizes that his prayer life is where everything else comes from: his success, his wholeness, the blessings for the day, the wisdom for the day, the ideas from God all come in prayer. In fact, the center of his intimacy with Christ revolves around the time he meets with Him. He can't wait to get back with Him. He perceives his prayer time as meeting a long-lost lover at the end of the day. He runs into the arms of his Father and grabs hold of Him as tight as he can. He shares his heart with Him and listens carefully to hear God's heart as He shares it with him.

The Father can't wait for prayer time with a mature believer because He has secrets He longs to share and He's waiting for somebody who's really listening and really cares about what He is saying. Jesus often said, *He who has ears to hear, let him hear* in His parables. He was saying, you can sit here and listen to this, but the only people who are going to get it are the people who really want to listen, people who really have ears to hear. In other words, you might sit through this, but you might not get it because you don't really want to hear it. Mature believers don't habitually forget their quiet time. They would be dead. It would be like saying, *"Oh, I forgot to eat for a week. I forgot to drink water for a week."* It would be like saying, *"Oh, I forgot to breathe for a week."* To a mature believer it is unthinkable.

In my late teen years, when I was about eighteen years old, I learned what Quiet Times were. Not because somebody taught them, but because I realized that I needed to spend time with God every day. There have been very, very few times that I have missed, that I have gone 24 hours without reading the Bible or separating myself from all the busyness of life just to pray.

DAY FIVE: MATURITY IS LEARNING HOW TO PERSEVERE IN EVERY AREA.

James 1:4: *Perseverance must finish its work so that you may be mature and complete, not lacking anything.*

We read this verse earlier in the book, but I want to reiterate it here because it talks about letting perseverance have its perfect work in you that you may become mature. In other words, in the process of building maturity in your life, you add one thing to another to another. Finally after you have done it all, learned the self-control and all these other areas we've talked about, perseverance is what makes it last. You make a decision to keep persevering until it perfects and refines you and you become mature.

Maturity is knowing how to persevere in every area. You persevere in resisting temptation. Some people think they have resisted in an area for a long time. But if they give in then they'll have to start all over again. They don't understand that part of growing and being mature is continuing to persevere.

You persevere in faith. Is there something you have been praying for that you know is the will of God, but you haven't seen it happen yet? Persevere in faith. You know your God. You know His Word. He says He wants to do this, so you persevere.

You persevere in prayer. When other people are playing, you are praying. Persevere in your quiet times. Persevere in memorizing Scripture. Persevere in longing after the deep things of God. Other people backslide. Other people fool around. Other people are having sex and going to parties. People in your youth group have bad attitudes and are not really wanting to grow, but you are persevering. You have to persevere. There is so much more of God that you have never tasted, that you have never discovered. How can you let go when you've just had one taste?

Are there things you need to persevere in? Are there areas where you've considered giving up?

_____

_____

_____

_____

I want you to take James 4:1 again and chew on it. Meditate on it and be that kind of person as you walk into your day today. Say, *"I'm going to be marked with maturity and I am going to persevere today. I am going to decide to be one of those Christians who perseveres when everybody else falls."* It may be hard. It's like running the wind sprints at the end of football practice. You want to fall down and wheeze to death, but you keep focused and you keep running. You keep pushing because you are going somewhere. You are going on to be like Jesus. You want to be a strong man or woman of God. You can't stop, you must persevere.

DAY SIX: IF YOU'RE GOING TO BE MATURE, YOU HAD BETTER GET READY TO PRESS ON.

Philippians 3:12-15: *Not that I have already obtained all this, or have already been made perfect, but I press on to take hold of that for which Christ Jesus took hold of me. Brothers, I do not consider myself yet to have taken hold of it. But one thing I do: Forgetting what is behind and straining toward what is ahead, I press on toward the goal to win the prize for which God has called me heavenward in Christ Jesus. All of us who are mature should take such a view of things. And if on some point you think differently, that too God will make clear to you.*

This is one of my all-time favorite Scriptures. This is the Scripture that kept me going through a lot of phases of my life. Write out what you think is the main point of this Scripture.

_____

_____

_____

_____

Paul is describing something he's done. He doesn't look at what's behind him—either failures or successes. He had great failures—he used to kill Christians. And he had great successes in planting churches all over the place. He says, *I don't look at those things. I keep pressing on. I keep going after the Lord with all of my guts. I let go of everything else. I am trying to figure out what God's purpose is for my life so I can go on to accomplish it.* Then he says that if they have a different mind, God would reveal that to them so they could be mature. He said, . . .*all the mature should take such a view of things.* In other words, if you are going to be mature, you better get ready to press on. You better get ready to keep running after the things of God even when you don't feel like it. There are going to be times when you feel like you're falling. There will be times when you don't feel like God is right next to you. You may not always feel the presence of God, but press on no matter what.

There are going to be times when you get to the top of a victory in your life, and you don't think you will ever fall. At that point, you need to press on. There are going to be times when you feel like you've failed God and all your friends and your family. You feel like you're at the bottom of a pit. At that time, you need to pick yourself up and press on. A mature believer presses on. A mature believer doesn't give up. What Paul is trying to get through to all of us is even though he did all the things he did—he planted churches, went on mission trips, was stoned, was shipwrecked—he never gave up. He never thought, *"Hey, I've arrived. I never need to do anything else."* He never gave up in any of his failures and said, *"I'm in jail. I can't do anything."* He said, *"I press on, I press on, I press on."* This needs to be a motto of the life of a mature believer. It needs to come off your lips on a regular basis. I'm going to press on. I don't care what people say, I'm going to press on. I don't care how discouraged I feel, I'm going to press on. I don't care how down I feel, I'm going to press on. I don't care how much church I've had, I'm going to press on. I don't care how much Bible I've read, I'm going to press on. There is more of God that I've not yet touched. I've only seen a glimpse of Him. Even though I've been saved for many years, I've barely got a taste of Him, and I want more.

Notice that pressing on does not come because there are people around you continually cheering you on. You don't always feel like pressing on. Pressing on means you get up, dust yourself off, and make yourself go after God with all of your heart on a regular basis. Why? Because you know that when you got on your knees and gave your life to Jesus for the first time, that was a right thing to do. And you know it was real, and God really forgave you and set you free and gave you a new heart. So you get back up and say, *"He's the one I'm running after and He's the one I'm pressing on for. I'm going to keep pressing on no matter what I have to go through. I want to see Him face to face."*

Write Philippians 3:12-15 on an index card. Take about five minutes right now to meditate on these verses. All day long think about pressing on no matter what happens.

DAY SEVEN: THESE ARE SIGNS OF MATURITY.

We have been talking all week long about signs of maturity in a believer's life. As you notice, we have put out some of the peripheral things that you always hear—don't do drugs, don't listen to secular music, don't have sex. You should be beyond those things now. We are talking about building a fortress of character in your life. That character is maturity. All the elements we have been talking about this week are sure signs that your faith is being refined and purified. You are no longer just an air-head, flighty little Christian.

Take some time right now and review all the Scriptures we have talked about this week. Meditate on them. Take three minutes on each Scripture and chew on it. This should take you eighteen minutes if you do that three minutes for each Scripture each day. Come on, you're a mature believer, you can do it. You want to grow—you can do it. Don't just skip over this part and go on to the next part. Stop right now and meditate on these Scriptures.

Eighteen minutes later. . . I want you to make a list of what you are going to do to implement some of these signs of maturity into your life. Now is the time to make some decisions that you are going to stick to forever. Do this now while your thinking is clear and coherent, while you have been going through this purifying, heart-raking process of growing closer to the Lord. Make some decisions and write them out right here. Make a declaration to God. Make a promise to go into maturity in these specific areas of your life.

_____

_____

_____

_____

_____

_____

Now pray over these and commit them to the Lord.

ACTION POINTS

What am I going to do in response to what I learned this week?

_____

_____

_____

_____

_____

_____

_____

_____

_____

_____

_____

_____

_____

WEEK TEN

....

GROWING UP EMOTIONALLY

DAY ONE: A MATURE CHRISTIAN DOESN'T PAY ATTENTION TO HIS EMOTIONS.

Our emotional life is probably one of the slowest areas for us to mature in as Christians. As children grow up, you see them learn to feed themselves, dress themselves, and go to the bathroom themselves. They may look like they are well adjusted, yet emotionally they are still very much developing. They cry at the drop of a hat, or someone might do something and they scream really loud.

When a young child cries because someone screams at him or pretends to be a monster, we might hold him and think, *"Oh, that's cute. What a soft and tender heart he has."* But if someone screams like a monster behind an eighteen-year-old and he breaks into tears, something is wrong with that person. He is not yet adjusted emotionally. It's not cute anymore.

Many Christians are like that. They go to church their whole life but they are very immature emotionally. The depth of their Christian life is only as deep as their emotions. These are the people who cry at the drop of a hat whenever there is an altar call. These are the people who just want to get together and hold hands or put their arms around each other and rock back and forth during a slow worship song. I can't tell you how many times I've seen young people grab their friends' hands during a worship service and pull together trying to have an emotional experience with each other rather than focusing on their relationship with God. When a song is sung to the Lord, it should be an intimate moment between the individual and God.

If we start relying on our emotions for our Christianity, then when we are emotionally up our Christianity will be up. And when we are emotionally down, our Christianity will be down. The Bible says we should be stable in all our ways. Proverbs 4:26 says, *Let all thy ways be established.* That is, we walk on an even keel. We are not hype-oriented Christians.

When we look at all of the gauges in our Christian life, we shouldn't even have an emotional gauge. Some people will look at their emotions and if they run high, then they'll really read their Bible, be close to God, and hang out with their Christian friends. But if their emotional tank is empty because they're looking at that gauge and they see that there is not much in it, then they won't do any of those things.

A mature Christian doesn't even measure, doesn't even pay attention to what his emotions are like to determine what his relationship with God should be like. He is looking at other gauges: *"How much Word have I read? How much have I prayed lately? How are my worship times? How much maturity have I seen develop in my life? How much growth have I had in the past week, in the past month of my life?"*

Take some time now to honestly answer those questions. How much time are you spending reading your Bible? How are your prayer times? Are you growing? How?

_____

_____

_____

_____

_____

Meditate on Proverbs 4:26 before you leave your Quiet Time today.

DAY TWO: DON'T LET YOUR WEARINESS GUIDE YOUR LIFE.

So much has happened in our society to mess up the emotions of young people. There have been physical, spiritual, and emotional abuse against too many young children. How many young people today are really hurting inside? There are those who have been beaten by their parents, who have been sexually abused, whose parents have been divorced, and whose parents have said things to make them feel like a "nothing" their whole life.

Jesus said, *Come to me, all you who are weary and burdened, and I will give you rest. Take my yoke upon you and learn from me, for I am gentle and humble in heart, and you will find rest for your souls. For my yoke is easy and my burden is light.* (Matthew 11:28-30). He said if you are weary or hurting or going through some tough times, then **come to me**—don't run from me. Don't let your weariness guide your life. Don't let all the bad things that have happened to you dictate how you live your life.

The areas of your life that still hurt are those you haven't dealt with yet and emotionally are stunting your growth. In other words, if you have really been hurt by someone and that part of your past is all you can think about, it's stunting your growth and keeping you from growing up. I want to encourage you today to take that part of your life and give it to the Lord. Ask the Lord to begin to heal up your broken heart and your wounded emotions. Pray a prayer of forgiveness to let go of that hurt and the memories that are trying to devour your future. You start growing up emotionally and becoming mature when you deal with hurts from the past.

Write out some of the hurts that you will deal with. Don't use this just to express your anger and bitterness. Only write out what you are really dealing with and letting go of. Then go to God with this list and let Him give you rest in your soul.

_____

_____

_____

Write Matthew 11:28-30 on an index card. Memorize it and meditate on it today and whenever the hurt gets too much.

DAY THREE: GUARD YOUR HEART.

Let's talk about boyfriend/girlfriend relationships today. The mark of a mature believer is that he is not easily sucked into new romantic flames. Some of you have arguments justifying why it's okay to go out with this guy or this girl. The fact is most of our brain is so foggy from our hormones that we don't really know what is going on. We think it is real love, but it's really just hormones going crazy because someone gave us a look or had a sparkle in her eye.

Part of growing up through adolescence is having all kinds of wild emotions anyway. It doesn't help that everybody else your age is going through wild emotions, too. You're starting to notice there are guys or girls who are interested in you.. But a mature believer sees past all that because he can see that the world has painted a picture in the minds of guys and girls, making them feel like they <u>need</u> to have each other, or they're just a loser. They feel like they must not be normal if they are not attached to someone of the opposite sex.

The Bible says, *Above all else, guard your heart, for it is the wellspring of life.* (Proverbs 4:23). A mature believer realizes that it might look fun, cool, and romantic. But getting involved in a relationship that's not a solid, mature, wholesome, godly romance can be letting your heart ultimately get infected by another person's heart who doesn't know the Lord or who isn't very close to the Lord.

You need to understand that I am <u>for</u> relationships, and I think romance is great. I have been married for thirteen years. Katie and I have a great romance which is the result of a wholesome friendship.

Teenagers all over the country are learning how to court instead of getting emotionally sucked into infatuation relationships where the heart gets broken again and again and again. Mature believers can see right through it when a guy or girl comes on to them. They are not impressed with muscles, money, cars, or popularity. They are only impressed with godliness, with fervor for God, with character in their life. Mature believers are only impressed with how much others have read the Bible lately, what God is doing with their life, and if they are really solid in the Lord. They don't want one of these hype-oriented Christians.

I want you to take Proverbs 4:23 and begin chew on it right now. Guard your heart. Take three minutes and meditate on it. Say it over and over again, until you're almost sick of it.

I know this touched the core of most teenagers. They think, "*Oh, we were doing great up to this point. We were growing in the Lord, and now you had to go bring this up. Why does it have to be so hard?*" Actually, it's not so hard; it's God protecting your heart from getting crushed again and again like the hearts of most people. I want you to take Proverbs 4:23 with you all day and meditate on it. Make a commitment to the Lord this morning that you want to see through all the worldly games. You want to become mature emotionally so you don't need to have a boyfriend or girlfriend to feel secure or confident about who you are. You get your confidence from God himself.

DAY FOUR: A MATURE CHRISTIAN SEEKS HELP AND DOES SOMETHING WITH THE HELP HE GETS.

Another sign of emotional and spiritual immaturity is being a leech Christian. These are people who are always trying to get somebody else's attention. They are very surfacey and always looking for security and attention. They rely on other people's strength to be strong. They always have a problem they need to tell you about. They are always trying to get the time and attention of a leader. Don't get me wrong, these leaders are there to lead you and to help you grow. But there are people who are always either depressed or going through a traumatic situation. They are calling the youth pastor in the middle of the night. They're just up and down emotionally, and they're a drain. Listen, if we're going to leech onto anybody, we need to leech onto Jesus. He's got enough energy and enough spiritual nourishment for all of us.

It's time for us to grow up. The spiritually immature person is somebody who wants the attention of the pastor or the youth pastor but won't spend any time in the Word. He doesn't spend any time in prayer or really worshipping God. While the youth pastor is preaching, he's just doodling and passing notes. What that tells me about that person is he is not serious about God. He just wants attention. He's immature. He meets with the youth pastor who says, *"Take this verse and meditate on it. Memorize it. It will help you."* He comes back two weeks later with the same problem, still depressed. The youth pastor asks, *"Have you done anything with that Scripture?"* He says, *"Oh, no. I didn't really feel like it."* He is more interested in attention than he's in getting real help. He is more interested in taking up time than in really developing himself. But if a mature believer has a problem he needs help with, he'll get help and then he'll do something with the help he gets. These are the people who are having quiet times, taking notes, and meditating on Scripture, but are still challenged with something. When they go and get some help from one of their leaders, they choose not to be a leech. They apply what they learn, and they put it in their life.

The Bible says in James that we should be not hearers only, but doers of the Word. James 1:22 says, *Do not merely listen to the word, and so deceive yourselves. Do what it says.* If you do this, it will keep you from being a leech Christian and spiritually sucking people dry.

Think now if you have any leech-like tendencies in your life at all. It's time to repent of that, and say, *"God I'm so sorry. I'm going to start crawling back to you. I'm going to come back to you and get my spiritual strength from your Word, from meeting with you. In Jesus name, Amen."*

Memorize James 1:22. Meditate today on actually doing what you've heard and read from God's Word, not just sitting back and listening.

DAY FIVE: AS A MATURE CHRISTIAN YOU NEED TO SEE THROUGH THE EMOTION OF THE MOMENT.

Part of growing up emotionally is learning to see what God wants to do in your life. What does God want to do in the lives of young people at the youth rally, camp, or convention you're attending? He doesn't want you getting sucked into the emotion of it.

A lot of people's Christianity is totally wrapped up in emotionalism. For example, whenever there is an altar call they want to go forward and pray and cry. So they keep going forward, whenever there is a call to commit or recommit their life to the Lord. They are already pretty committed. They just are going down for another emotional rush. I've seen people come forward on the Friday night of an *Acquire the Fire* to recommit their life to Jesus and then come forward on Saturday night to recommit their life again. What it tells me is they are not emotionally mature. They are sucked into an emotional moment. They pull their friends with them and say, *"Let's just go down there and cry together and pray."* Listen, this is what keeps people babies in Christ. They want another special moment, and they don't really want to grow.

I remember after I had been a Christian for just a year or two, a friend of mine who was standing next to me in church said, *"Do you want to go forward and pray, just to experience the moment."* I just looked at him and said, *"No."* I was already saved. I wasn't living in sin. I was committed. He was, too. I wasn't fallen away in any area. I just didn't think there was any sense in going forward again. That's not being a spiritual giant, it's just being a coherent Christian and not an air head.

So you're at a big meeting and there are thousands of people there. There is a great plea to recommit your life, but you're already as committed as you know how to be. There is no sin in your life. Maybe the plea is not even speaking to your heart that much because you feel pretty committed to the Lord. Yet something compels you to go down there. What is that? It could be the Spirit of God, or it could be your emotions getting stirred up. I would challenge you to think it through. What is the preacher saying? What is the altar call for? Why is he asking people to come forward? Does it apply to your life? What change do you want to see in your life as a result of going forward? An emotionally mature Christian will see through the emotionalism of an altar call and see what God is wanting him to do with the decision that He wants him to make. Ephesians 5:10 says, *"Find out what pleases the Lord."*

I was at a Newsboys concert not long ago where there were probably about ten thousand Christians. They were excited, jumping, screaming, and singing along with all the songs. Then someone came out to preach. As the altar call was given he said, *"All those who want to receive the love of God and know you're going to heaven, come forward right now."* Probably 6,000 teenagers came to the front. Something is not right. All ten thousand of these kids were jumping and screaming and singing along with the Newsboys songs. That means they must be in church, they must know Jesus, they must be listening to this music. Yet all these kids are going forward now to "receive the love of Jesus, and go to heaven." Well I have to admit, some of the fault of emotionalism is on the part of the preachers. Some of them play the music just right and get their lights just right, but don't really care about what they are asking. They just want an emotional moment. They want to see people respond. They want to see people get down there and cry. It's sad to say, but it's true. You need to see through that as a mature believer. Again, you need to think it through: *"Wait a minute, I don't need to go forward on this. God's already done this in my life. If I'm gong to go forward, I'm not going to cry just because everybody else cries. I'm not going to just put my arms around my friends and try to make a moment out of it. I want to see if God is really doing something in my life."*

Sometimes preachers are guilty of drawing people into a moment like this by being broad and not specific. So if you're standing in the audience you could be thinking, *"Okay, well, yeah, I want to know I'm going to heaven, and I want to accept the love of God. Yeah,*

I'm already saved, but I want to accept more of His love, so I guess I should go forward. So am I committing myself for the first time, or am I recommitting myself? Do I do what I did before? I don't know, I'm just going forward for an emotional moment." As a mature believer you need to see through the emotions of the moment. Don't just go forward because thousands of others are going. If God's really doing something in your life, yes, go for it! But don't let your youth group drag you along for an emotional moment, and don't you drag them along for an emotional moment. This is not about emotion. Yes, salvation affects our emotions, but it's not all emotions. It will stir up your emotions, but what's more important is what God is wanting to do in your life at that moment.

Think through sermons you've heard the past three or four months. Were there any where the altar call seemed to be more emotionalism? Sometimes stories will draw on emotions. Sometimes it's the preacher who's crying will draw on emotions. It's more important to consider the Word of God that he or she is speaking on. What is God wanting to do in your life? If you want to respond to that call, then that's the reason to go forward, whether everybody is going forward or no one is going forward. Think about it before you have the opportunity to hear your next sermon.

Memorize and meditate on Ephesians 5:10 until it's really deep in your heart. Then the next time you hear an altar call, you can examine your heart to make sure your going forward would really please the Lord.

DAY SIX: AS A MATURE CHRISTIAN THERE WILL BE TIMES YOU'LL NEED TO ENCOURAGE YOURSELF IN THE LORD.

Turn for a moment to 1 Samuel 30:1-6. Take a few minutes to read it. I want to draw your attention to another sign of an emotionally mature Christian. Let me give you the scenario David was in the middle of. Everything was going wrong when he was off attacking other cities. People came in and attacked his city and took everything away as well as all the wives, families, children. When David's men came back, they were mad. At first they were sad and cried. Then they got mad at David. They wanted to stone him. Think about the situation. These were the guys he had discipled, guys he had ministered to. They were his buddies, his pals. They had been winning wars together all around the region, and now they wanted to stone him, to kill him. He was at the end of his rope. He was backed into a corner. He didn't have anybody to turn to. Let me tell you something, you are going to find yourself the same way. There are going to be times in your life, even in your teenage Christian life, where you don't have anybody to turn to. People who were your best friends, even your best Christian friends, will turn against you or away from you. They're really not looking for the Lord anymore, or they're not as on fire as they used to be, or as you are. People you thought were on your side now want to persecute you or are talking about you. You have to decide what you're going to do. If you are emotionally immature, you may just say, *"Well I can't handle it. It's not my fault. I'm going to lay down and let them run all over me."* But this is not what David did. He went to the Lord and he found strength. Another translation says, *he encouraged himself.* There are going to be times when you're going to have to go and encourage yourself. You're going to have to grab hold of the Word of God. Grab your Bible and get alone. Grab hold of all that Word of God you've been meditating on, memorizing and putting down in your heart, and go get alone with God.

We can't be emotionally crippled Christians who are trying to get other people to hold us up all the time, or we're just going to fall down and fall all to pieces. We have to be men and women who will stand up and do what is right, even if it's hard. Even if we're hurting, we must be the ones who are willing to stand. Even if we feel like we're all alone and all our friends who say they're Christians have let us down, we need to go off and get tight with God. If you can't find anybody else to encourage you, you have to encourage yourself. You must exhort yourself. Go let the Word of God minister to you. Go get alone with God and fill yourself up. Let me tell you something, when you start developing that kind of Christianity, you've just grown into a whole other level. You've just separated the men from the boys. You've just decided that you refuse to be a mamby-pamby, thumb-sucking baby Christian the rest of your life. Now this is the kind of Christian Jesus is looking for. He wants people who will say, *"Enough is enough. I'm not in this thing for hype. I'm not in this thing to be a leech. I'm in this to grow up, to become all that God has called me to be as a man or a woman of God."*

I want you to find an opportunity to go and encourage yourself. Build yourself up even when no one else is building you up. I want you to get in the habit of encouraging yourself. Start purposing in your heart to take some time every day to go and encourage yourself in the Lord. No matter what you are doing. Go between a couple classes at school, right in the middle of the heat of the battle. Go when you're right in the middle of trying to make a decision about some important issue or about some peer pressure issue. Just escape from everything and go get encouraged. If you do this, then you'll be on your way to solid footing in your walk with God the rest of your life.

Take some time now to memorize 1 Samuel 30:6, *But David found strength in the Lord his God.* Meditate on it today all day long. Think about the strength you can only find in God—not in your friends, family, or pastors—only in the Lord your God.

DAY SEVEN: GROWING UP EMOTIONALLY.

Wow! What a week. Growing up in emotions is something that most of us never hear much about. As a result, we are far away from all the blessings in our life that God wants us to have. Growing up emotionally doesn't happen by just reading one chapter a week in this devotional. Maybe you've just discovered this week that you're really not very mature emotionally. Go back through the Scriptures we studied this week and chew on them.

Begin dealing with areas where you are challenged in your life today. Make decisions about how you're going to continue to grow up emotionally and not be swayed by the buttons people can push in you, or by your past, or by your emotions. Decide that you will only be swayed the Word of God. Decide now to grow to up emotionally. Begin to apply the Word of God in your life. Think through the surface emotionalism that you have been walking and living in as a Christian so far. Refuse to stay a baby the rest of your life.

ACTION POINTS

What am I going to do in response to what I learned this week?

_____

_____

_____

_____

_____

_____

_____

_____

....

MATURE FIRE FOR GOD

DAY ONE: GOD IS NOT LOOKING FOR A FLICKER OR A SPARK, BUT A MATURE FIRE.

Many teenage Christians are totally emotionally driven and hype-oriented. They get hyped up about this and hyped up about that. They use the words *"on fire for Jesus"* like they are cheering at a ball game. Our God is not looking for a flicker or a spark but for a mature fire in their lives. He's looking for fervor, a yearning after the deep things of God that makes you different from every other human being on the face of this earth who is not totally in love with God.

Deuteronomy 4:24 says, *For the LORD your God is a consuming fire, a jealous God..* The Bible says God is a fire. He doesn't have some fire; His very Presence is fire. He showed Himself this way with Moses in the burning bush. He used fire over and over again throughout the Bible in a symbolic way of representing himself. God is real. You can't grab Him and put Him in your pocket. It's like the realness of the burning flames of a fire. You put your hand into it, you know it is hot, but you can't hold it. God has specifically designed our hearts to be the only thing that can "hold" His fire. Jesus said in Luke 12:49, *I have come to bring fire on the earth.* He didn't come to bring rules or regulations. He didn't come to bring rituals. He didn't come so you could have a nice little Bible Club. He didn't come so you could have some fun at youth group. He came to bring the fire of His Father's Presence. . .the fire that was in the burning bush. . .the fire that was on Mount Sinai when Moses went to meet with God. It's that same fire from the Presence of the Father that Jesus came to bring to your heart and your life. Do you dare to have enough guts to receive His fire?

Many people have prayed their little prayer and then gone to church their whole life, but they have no fire in their lives. You look in their eyes and they look just as dead as the world does. They'll say, *"Oh, yeah, I just love the Lord with all my heart, my soul, and my strength."* But they say it like it's some kind of dreary drudgery that they're forced to put themselves through, rather than an explosive fire that has set their heart free.

This morning I want you to begin to have a heart that's hungry for the fire of God. Develop a heart that is calling out to the Lord. Don't just go through the motions. Desire the reality of His Presence in your life today. Begin praying, *"Lord, I know Your Word says You are a fire. So Lord, if You are a fire, and Your Word says You live within me, ignite my heart with Your fire."* I want you to take the next four minutes to chew on Deuteronomy 4:24 and Luke 12:49. Say them over and over until they light up your heart and become reality to you. Don't leave your Quiet Time to start your day until you've got the fire in your heart.

DAY TWO: MANY CHRISTIANS WALK AROUND CARRYING DEAD BRANCHES.

Yesterday we learned that the Bible says our God is a consuming fire. To consume means to eat up, to dispose of. The first thing God wants to consume is all the garbage in our lives. Turn to John 15 and read verses 1-6. Note what verse 6 says, *If anyone does not remain in me, he is like a branch that is thrown away and withers; such branches are picked up, thrown into the fire and burned.* Any branch that does not remain in Christ dies. A dead branch is only good for one thing—to be cut off and burned. This is a perfect picture of what God wants to do in our lives. He wants to burn parts of our lives that have not remained in Christ—attitudes, habits, and sin. He wants to consume those things. He wants to burn them out of our lives. He wants us to cut off those dead branches.

Many Christians have been walking around for a long time carrying those dead branches. They go to church with dead branches. They go to school with dead branches. They go everywhere with dead branches, acting as if nothing is wrong. The dead branches are the sin they carry around with them. . .the bad attitudes, fooling around with sex and immorality, drugs and drinking. People cry, *"Lord, where are you? I don't feel very close to you"* while all the time they are carrying around dead branches. If you want God's presence to be real to you, the first thing He wants to say to you is, *"Let me burn the garbage out of your life."* Many of us want the benefits of Christianity—being close to God and hearing His voice—but not enough are willing to pay the price to get that benefit. The price is letting Him burn the sin out of your life.

How do you cut a branch off? You repent. You make a decision to ask God to forgive you in that area and to cut that part of your life off. Don't allow yourself to be a slave to that sin anymore. On the following page, make a list right here of some areas of your life that need to be cut off.

_____

_____

_____

_____

_____

_____

_____

_____

Make the decision right now to repent and cut those things off. Prepare to have them burned out of your life.

Now, when something is burned, you can't go back and use it later because all you have left are ashes. You can't take a sin and hide it. You can't say, *"Well, I'm just going to take this alcohol and hide it for awhile. I'll repent, but if I ever backslide, then I'll have it again when I need it."* When you let God cut it off and burn it, it's gone forever. Determine now that it is impossible to go back. Don't make any provisions for yourself to be able to get back to that old sin. Let God begin to burn the garbage out of your life, even this morning. Repent of this stuff and you'll sense His Presence in your life all day long in a way you have never known.

DAY THREE: GOD WANTS TO BE THE PASSION OF YOUR HEART.

The most important thing is that God wants to consume our heart with a passionate love for Him. He wants to be the One who overwhelms your heart. He wants to be what causes your heart to beat fast in the morning when you get up, thinking *"God, I can't wait to meet with You today."* He wants to be what thrills you most. He wants to be the passion of your heart and the passion of your life.

The Bible says, *Love the Lord your God with all your heart and with all your soul and with all your mind and with all your strength.* (Mark 12:30). Those aren't just some cheesy, boring words. It's really what God wants. It's really the kind of love He wants—the very core of who we are wrapping ourselves around Him.

David said it like this: *As the deer pants for streams of water, so my soul pants for you, O God.* (Psalm 42:1). God, You really are the love of my life. You know when someone's heart is on fire for someone else. When you see a guy or a girl who is infatuated with somebody, that is all he or she can talk about. Talk. . .talk. . .talk. He talks about her so much that he becomes obnoxious and people don't want to be around him. Finally you get so irritated you just yell, *"Shut up. Quit talking about her so much! Find something else to talk about!"*

The Bible says that out of the abundance of your heart the mouth speaks (Matthew 12:34). In other words, you are going to talk about whatever is going on in your heart . When was the last time someone told you to shut up because you were talking about God too much? It's a good way to measure what is going on in your heart. If your heart is consumed with a passionate love and fervent yearning to go after Him with all your heart, with all you are as a person, it is going to come out of your mouth. You can't help it. If you have a problem talking about God, stop thinking about your lips for a while and start thinking about your heart. Is the Lord God really the consuming fire in your heart? Are you letting Him eat up every part of your life? When you meet with Him in the morning do you just slam on the brakes and say *"Oh, Lord, I just want to stop and love You this morning, and I want to let You love me this morning. Lord, I want You to eat away every part of my heart. Lord, consume every part of my life. Be the compelling force that drives me to my knees all day long."*

Stop right now. Get on your knees. Take Mark 12:30 and Psalm 42:1 and begin to say them to the Lord. *"Lord, I do love You with all my heart. Lord, as the deer pants for the water, yes my soul does long for You."* And if you can't say it with a true heart, just break down and say, *"God, don't let my heart be hard."* Break the hardened shell and the callousness that has been around you, and say, *"God, I want Your fire to burn a hole right through my heart. Lord, let me not go through the motions one more day pretending like a petrified Christian. I want the fiery presence of Your love burning in my life today."*

Don't you dare leave for your day until you have it.

DAY FOUR: YOU NEED TO RID YOURSELF OF THE THINGS
THAT KEEP YOUR FIRE FROM BEING LIT.

This morning let's talk about why some matches don't light.
Many times we say, *"God, I want you to light my heart on fire,"* but we
don't understand why it doesn't light. We ask for it flippantly and
quickly and nothing seems to happen. Let's look at matches. There
are a lot of reasons matches don't light.

They are all wet.

Have you ever dropped matches in a puddle of water, then picked
them up real quick hoping they were not all wet? You grab one that you
think is the driest and try to light it, but it doesn't light. . .doesn't light.
. .doesn't light. Wet matches won't light just like a wet heart won't light.

Have you been submerged in the world for so long that it is hard
for God to light you? Maybe you cut off a branch that is sin in your life,
but you've been trying to get that branch green gain by putting it in
water. You've got dead wood, but it's wet inside so God can't light it.

Some of us have been submerged in the world for so long that
we repel fire. When we are around worldly music, worldly TV, worldly movies, worldly friends all the time we are submerged in the
water. Occasionally we come up for a second to get a gasp of air at
Youth Group every week or at church on Sunday, but then we go
back under the water. We cry and we wonder why we're not on fire.
What's wrong? Are you submerged? Are you wet? Is your heart wet?
Maybe if you would come up *out of the world* long enough then God
could really light you on fire.

Old matches don't light.

Ever grab matches that has been sitting in your drawer for ten
years and try to light one and the end crumbles off? Is that how your
faith is? Maybe you've been in church your whole life. You prayed a
prayer when you were a kid, and now it's just old to you. *"Yeah, yeah,
yeah. I heard this sermon before. I heard this Scripture before."* If we're
not careful, we can become arrogant and cocky, thinking we've heard

everything there is to hear about Jesus. We think we know all there is to know. How could it be? We know one billionth of one speck of what there is to know about God and we think we've heard it all before.

Has your faith grown kind of "old"? Has your Christianity grown "old"? Not mature, just "old," like "old hat" to you? If that is you this morning, just say, *"God, I'm sorry. I've been in touch with religion and tradition, but I haven't connected with You. My faith is old. I know You're not boring or dry. God, break the hardness of my oldness and my callousness because I want to be on fire."*

Matches can't light in the wind.

Have you ever seen someone try to light a match and to keep it lit to light something else, like a cigarette or a campfire, when it's windy? They light it and then protect it in the cup of their hand, but it still goes out. Then they gather their friends around them to try to shield the wind, but it still goes out. They hide behind a corner and it still goes out because you can't light a match in the wind.

So many of us try to get on fire for God. God touches our life at a camp or conference and then we go back into the world. We get blown on by the devil. Peer pressure and temptation blows out our fire. Then we go back to God saying, *"I guess it wasn't real. I guess that what I thought was Your fire was just emotionalism."*

No, it's not just emotions. It's a real fire. It's a real touch of the presence of the living God. You just got back into the world and let the world blow your fire out. If you are going to have a mature fire in your heart, you have to learn to give God a chance to work in your life. For fifteen, sixteen, seventeen years the world has been setting its fire in your heart. Don't just give God five seconds at an altar call thinking that will make it last forever.

When you go back into the world and the world blows out what you thought was real, you start to wonder if it really was. You have to separate yourself from the world long enough for God to set a raging fire in your heart. It has to be long enough to burn all the garbage out. Let it burn long enough to really grab hold of all your attention. Sure He does it for a second during the ministry time; you have to make sure it will last.

Maybe you've had a fire in your heart for God in the past, but it has blown out. Maybe you're discouraged. Are you just praying for five minutes and wondering why God doesn't do anything? Wait a minute, you've been in the world all these years, now you have to give God some time to keep the fire raging in your heart.

Have you been throwing yourself back into the "wind" of the world and getting blown out? It's time to make a decision: Separate yourself. Only hang around Christian friends. Only have godly influences in your life. Shut off the TV. Shut off the secular music. Let God's fire begin to rage strong in your heart and become a mature fire.

Connect with the striker.

Have you ever seen somebody try to light a match without watching what he is doing so he is rubbing the match against the cardboard but not the striker? You can't light a match when it's not connecting to the striker.

Many Christians do all the "right things," wear Christian T-shirts, go to youth group, go to youth camp. They have all the outward signs of Christianity, but they never connect with the striker. They never just sit down and get real with God. You need to connect with God Almighty. You need to shut off all your Christian rituals (the things you do to look real spiritual), and you need to connect with the Lord Jesus and His Father.

This morning before you leave your quiet time, connect with the striker. Say, *"God, right now, I'm going to wait on You. I'm asking you to light up my heart."*

DAY FIVE: TO KEEP THE FIRE GOING, YOU MUST CONTINUE TO USE THE SAME INGREDIENTS THAT GOT YOUR FIRE GOING IN THE FIRST PLACE.

One of the things that happens when young people leave a camp, a conference, or a missions trip all on fire for God is they don't think it's possible to have the same fire at home. They think it was just an amazing thing that God did, but there's no way they can keep the same fire. Well, I tell you that is a lie.

I got on fire for God when I was sixteen years old. I dropped all the garbage and sin that I was doing. I'm not perfect, but I've never intentionally turned my back on God and said *"No, I don't want You anymore, Lord."*

When people hear me say that, they think I must be some spiritual giant. They think I must know all these big, profound secrets. How can I keep my fire when hardly anyone else does? Well, let me tell you the secret right here this morning. If you want a mature fire, a fire that lasts and keeps burning and burning and burning, all you have to do is do the same things you did to get your fire started in the first place. Think about the camp or the conference—what was it that ignited your fire in that ministry environment?

It's like baking a cake. If you put all the right ingredients in, the cake will always turn out well. But if you put everything but the eggs in, it won't turn out right. If you put everything but the sugar in, it won't turn out right. It is the same way with our fire for God. If you put together the same ingredients that got the fire going, you will keep the fire going. If you leave one thing out, it's not going to be the same. Think about the ingredients that first ignited your heart for God when you were at that camp or convention.

No TV's and movies - When you're at a camp or a retreat you probably aren't watching any television or seeing any movies. You aren't being entertained by some outside force. You are secluded from any worldliness invading your mind. You might say you can't help it. You just automatically turned on the TV. Yes you can help it.

You can shut it off. You can go in the other room. You don't have to let that stuff feed you worldliness. It can drown out what God is wanting to speak to you. The principle in operation is that during that time you secluded yourself from the garbage of the world so you could really hear from God. And because you shut the worldliness off, you could hear God better. Think about it. You did it once, now do it at home.

No Secular music - At most camps or any kind of ministry experience where God is really moving, young people are not allowed to listen to or bring any secular music with them. Again, it is amazing what happens when you shut off the worldly influence from your life. You can begin to hear God's voice. The confusion and all the voices of the world are muffled so you can hear what the God of the universe is trying to say to you. What you are doing by shutting off the music and by shutting off the movies is preparing your fireplace for a fire. You are preparing yourself and setting yourself up for a move of God in your life.

Worship - Usually wherever you've seen God really light young people's hearts on fire, there's been a great environment of worship. It's amazing how many people really worship God at camp or at a conference, then go back to church and just "sing songs"—just clap their hands and sing without thinking about the words—instead of really worshipping. Think of what worship was like while you were at that camp. God was the most supreme thing in your mind while you were singing. Your eyes were closed, and you were singing as loud and strong as you could, worshipping God. If you want to have the same fire for God that you had at that time, then do the same things you did while you were there. Close your eyes during your quiet time. Begin to sing out and worship God with all your heart. Next time you go to church or youth group, go ahead and cut loose and sing with everything in you.

Christian friends - When you are at that Christian retreat, you're surrounded by Christian friends the whole weekend. People are loving God. God is changing their lives. God is changing your life. You're talking about what God is doing or wants to do. You're dreaming together. You're thinking together. You're crying together. Now surround yourself with Christian friends again. You may say, *"I'm around all these heathens all day long at school."* Well, that's fine. But your best friends ought to be those who really love God. It's one of the ingredients that helped the fire start in your life to begin with. Make your Christian friends your very best friends.

If any of these ingredients are missing from your life, I want you to take a few minutes this morning and put them back into your life. Make a commitment in all four of these areas to keep these ingredients in your life today.

In Psalm 119:164, David says, *Seven times a day I stop to praise you.* Why don't you try that today. Seven different times stop for three or four minutes and just shut everything off. Say, *"God, You are awesome. You are incredible. I love You. I worship You."* Seven times today find an opportunity to do that. Keep these ingredients in your life and watch the fire burn strong.

DAY SIX: INGREDIENTS THAT GET AND KEEP YOUR FIRE BURNING.

Let's talk some more about the ingredients that help get your fire started and then keep it burning strong.

The Word of God - So there you were at camp hearing the Bible preached over and over again. You were talking among your friends about what was just preached and what God was speaking to you. You are hearing Scriptures quoted and ministered to you about what they really mean. How much of the Word of God do you hear on a regular basis now? It's one of the ingredients that helped set your heart on fire to begin with. People don't really understand why their fire is out. All they have to do is the same things they did to get their fire going. One of those things is staying in the Word of God. I'm not just talking about reading your one obligatory Scripture in the morning and that will do. I'm talking about chewing on it all day long. You hear us talking about the Word of God over and over again throughout this whole book because I know that it will keep your fire burning strong. Dive into it today.

Prayer - Think about prayer. After a while, a lot of people just go through the motions of having their quiet time or praying. It's important for you to pray the same way you did when you first got the fire of God in your life. Pour out your heart to God. Let Him know everything that's going on. Be real with Him. If you're having a problem, pour it out and let Him hear about it, man. He'll help you. He'll minister to you. He'll encourage you. If you're having a problem dealing with a situation in your life with another person, pray and let God know. Find out what His Word says about that situation and pray what His Word says, which is His will for that situation. Don't just be a petrified Christian chanting the same words with no life to them. Pour out your heart and pray with earnestness the same way you did when the fire started. You will be amazed at how strong the fire will stay.

Ministry to others - There you are at camp and you go forward with one of your friends who just got saved or has recommitted his life or is struggling in some area. You are praying with him and ministering to him, maybe crying with him. After that experience you thought, *"Wow, that was awesome. That was amazing. God used me and I saw some real change in my friend's life."* Ministering to other people is another ingredient to keep your fire burning. You need to reach out and have a heart of compassion for others. You should know what it feels like for God to use you on a regular basis. It shouldn't be only once a year at camp or at a conference. It shouldn't be just when you go on a mission trip somewhere. If you are constantly sensing God flowing through you to minister to other people and you see the change in their lives as a result, then you will begin to realize again that God really is real. It is amazing what He will do in a person's life, and He will use you to do it. It keeps your fire burning. Ministry is one of the essential ingredients. If you want to have a mature fire and not just a hype-kind of Christianity, you better stay involved in ministry to others.

Jeremiah 20:9 says, *But if I say, 'I will not mention him or speak any more in his name,' his word is in my heart like a fire, a fire shut up in my bones.*

I want you to write down a few names of people you see in class, or wherever you will be, who you can minister to today. Maybe they are saved and they need encouragement. Maybe they are not saved and you can say a few words which would penetrate their hearts. Write their names here and pray over these people today.

_____

_____

_____

_____

_____

_____

DAY SEVEN: MATURE FIRE FOR GOD.

We've been talking all week about having a mature fire, a fire that rages out of control for the things of God and not something that can be easily blown out. I want you to prepare your heart to be a fervent, passionate Christian. How do you get the fire lit in your heart? It's just like lighting a fire in the fireplace. Your heart is the fireplace where God wants to light you with His consuming fire.

Prepare your fireplace. Prepare your heart. Get all the deadwood and put it in the fireplace. Say, *"God, get ready to burn me."* This is something you should go through every day. Open yourself up and say, *"Lord, burn out the garbage in my life. I repent of anything that I did today or in the past that is not pure and not right in Your sight."* Prepare your heart. Is it really ready to have a fire, or do you have a lot of water and green wood in there? You can't light a fire in a fireplace that has water and green wood in it. You have to have dry wood, something that has been cut off and you don't want in your life anymore.

Connect with the striker. Let God light you, *"God, I'm not moving until You light me."* Are you thinking about all these ingredients we talked about that keep your heart flaming for God? Good. Think hard about them. Pray about them. Say *"God, I'm going into my day and into my life with all of these ingredients. I might be in this world, but I don't have to be like the world. I might have to go to a school where very few love You, but I don't have to be like everybody else there. I might be surrounded by people who aren't Christian, but I'm going to choose what to surround my heart with. I'm going to keep my heart submerged in the ingredients that keep my fire raging for You because I don't want to get blown out."* This need not be a one-day commitment, or a one-week commitment. This needs to be the position and the attitude of your heart every day before you leave your quiet time.

"Lord, I want to prepare my heart for the fire. And now, Lord, I want to connect with the striker. Consume my heart. God, I want the fire to fall on my life the same way the fire fell Elijah called it down. Lord, I want to call the fire of Your Presence down into my life before I

leave today. I want people to look in my eyes and look in my life and say 'What is it about you? What have you got? Who is it that you are in love with? There must be something going on inside of you.' That's right. I'm in love with my Creator. I'm in love with the One who sent His Son to die for me because He loved me so much."

When your heart is captured with love and fervor for God like that, you won't have to shove anything down anybody's throat. Just let it ooze out of you, and they'll want what you have.

Stop right now. Slam on the brakes. Connect with the striker. Review all the Scripture we read this week that talks about fire. Make sure you have them all written on index cards so you can meditate on them even when you're not at home in your quiet time.

Take these three ingredients into your day today and prepare for your heart to get ignited.

ACTION POINTS

What am I going to do in response to what I learned this week?

_____

_____

_____

_____

_____

_____

_____

_____

WEEK TWELVE

....

MATURITY = I AM NOT IN THE CENTER

DAY ONE: SELFISHNESS IS A SIGN OF IMMATURITY, WHILE SELFLESSNESS IS A SIGN OF STRENGTH AND GROWTH.

Most newborn babies become the center of attention. Everyone "oohs" and "aahs" at the sight of a newborn. All the attention is on this brand new human being. Everybody caters to the baby, feeds the baby, changes the baby, dresses the baby, and coos over the baby. Soon he learns that he is the center of her own world. Everyone waits on this newborn hand and foot, and rightly so, because the baby can't do it by himself.

As the child begins to grow, her parents know that it is not proper to always wait on her. She needs to learn to grow up and wait on herself a little bit at a time. Parents who don't teach their children this principle have very self-centered, "me-oriented" children. They are eight years old and still say things like, *"Where is my food?"* Or, *"Why didn't you do this for me?" "Why didn't you do that for me?"* All of us have seen spoiled children like that, and no one enjoys being with them. That behavior is appropriate for a baby but not for somebody who is growing up.

This also applies to our Christian life. When we are babies in Christ, everything is "me" oriented: How I feel, how I'm going to be blessed, how Jesus saved me. As you get your fire started and become stronger in the Lord, you need to understand how much Jesus loves you. How He wants to fill you, feed you, and nurture you. You need to be around people who can constantly lift you and develop you as a man or a woman of God.

As you continue to grow up, it's time to quit being so "me" centered—everything shouldn't revolve around you. Our society is made up of very selfish people who are only concerned with "me," "mine," and "my." People are always thinking about "my fun," "my comfort," "my reputation," "my image," "my friends," "my car," "my bedroom," "my stuff." We concentrate on how "I" look. It's always me, me, me. But as we grow up and mature as believers, there are some things that need to change.

As we all know, I Corinthians 13 is the love chapter. It talks about everything that someone who has the love of God in his heart should be doing and how he should be acting. I Corinthians 13:11 says, *When I was a child, I talked like a child, I thought like a child, I reasoned like a child. When I became a man, I put childish ways behind me..* When I was a child I was self-centered, I did childish things. But now that I have grown up a little bit I've matured, and I have learned how to love other people instead of just paying attention to myself. I have put away childish actions.

Selfishness is a sign of immaturity, but selflessness is a definite sign of strength and growth. I want you to list a few areas of your life where you have been selfish, concentrating only on yourself and not those around you:

_____

_____

_____

_____

I want you to pray over these things and make a decision to put away "childish things." Repent and say, *"I'm sorry for being self-centered. I'm going to begin to be others-centered."* Begin to be love centered. Think how you can love others, instead of just how you can take care of your own needs.

DAY TWO: PREFERRING OTHERS IS WHAT SELFLESSNESS IS ALL ABOUT.

The Bible talks about preferring others, about preferring one another. Read Romans 12:10 and Philippians 2:3. Preferring others is part of what loving selflessly is about. It is a sign of a mature believer. It's not just thinking about your own needs but also thinking about the needs of others. If it is a choice between your preference or theirs, prefer them. Let them choose. They may be more immature than you are. They need to know that there's somebody out there who cares about them as an individual. Maybe you're dealing with a new believer or maybe somebody who is not even saved. Your preferring them shows them that you are no longer self-centered, and that blows their mind because most of this world is self-centered.

I want you to think about some people or situations you will face today where you will have the opportunity to prefer another person. Write down their names right now and how you are going to prefer them over yourself today.

_____

_____

_____

_____

_____

_____

_____

Now, pray over their names and prepare to show that you're maturing as a believer by preferring others.

Look up Romans 12:10 and Philippians 2:3. Memorize and meditate on one—or both! Write them on an index card and carry them with you today.

DAY THREE: A MATURE CHRISTIAN WANTS OTHERS TO BE BLESSED AND DOES NOT BECOME JEALOUS OF THEIR STUFF.

I Corinthians 3:2-3: *I gave you milk, not solid food, for you were not yet ready for it. Indeed, you are still not ready. You are still worldly. For since there is jealousy and quarreling among you, are you not worldly? Are you not acting like mere men?*

What Paul is saying in the above Scripture is that jealousy and quarreling are signs of immaturity and self-centeredness. Jealousy is to desire something for yourself, not wanting anyone else to have it. This happens because you think you are more important than the other person. Quarreling is saying that you care only about your opinion, your own perspective. You know that you're right and anyone who disagrees with you is wrong. But as a mature believer who is selfless, you rejoice when others have something better than you. You're happy when others are blessed with a car or a stereo or new clothes. Instead of being envious or jealous, you're happy for them. You are genuinely joyful and willing to listen when they have something to say that's different from your point of view.

I've watched other people in youth ministries grow, get a new offices or a piece of land to build their facility. I've made a conscious decision not to be jealous, but to be thankful and grateful. Actually many times we have sent them a gift or money to help with their project. Instead of getting jealous, I've rejoiced with them and prayed for God to bless them.

Many people feel they have to be right all the time—and they're ready to fight to prove their point. But a mature believer who really wants other people to be blessed doesn't get jealous of their stuff. It really doesn't matter to him whether he's right or wrong. What's more important is that we have peace and that God is lifted up in every situation. (See Romans 12:18)

I want you to take a few minutes and chew on I Corinthians 3:2,3. Now think about some areas in your life where you have been jealous or quarreling and stirring up dissension among others. Write those areas down:

_____

_____

_____

_____

_____

_____

Now take some time to repent of those actions. Take this Scripture with you all day. Chew on it every time you feel like you are going to get jealous or want to quarrel with somebody. And when you find a person of whom you are jealous or with whom you want to quarrel, find a way to do the very opposite of what they expect you to do. This time show that you're growing and that you're a believer and no longer "me" centered.

DAY FOUR: A MATURE CHRISTIAN SEEKS TO LOVE, TO SERVE, AND TO GIVE.

Romans 13:8: *Let no debt remain outstanding, except the continuing debt to love one another, for he who loves his fellowman has fulfilled the law.* Another sign of maturity that goes along with the message of the first day of this week is whether we are more concerned about loving other people than being loved by them. The Bible says here that we owe other people love—whether we know them or not, whether we like them or not, whether we agree with them or not. When somebody comes to visit your youth group, and you feel strange not knowing what to say or do, you need to show that person love. Why? Because Jesus gave love to you first. He has put His love inside your heart so you are a debtor to that person. Before you ever met him you owed him something.

It is time to pay up. It's time to pay your bills. Somebody who's growing as a mature believer realizes he owes the world love. He doesn't seek to be loved, but he seeks to love. He doesn't seek to be served, he seeks to serve. He doesn't seek to receive, he seeks to give. In fact, he lives to give. He wants to give his life, his heart, his energy, his strength, and his love away to other people. The very opposite of being "me" centered is being "others" centered. It's showing that "I" don't have to be first in everything. In fact, you notice yourself very little because you are putting so much attention on others.

Take Romans 13:8 with you. Meditate on it all day long. Think about people you owe love to, maybe you haven't shown love to for a while or people you are going to meet today whom you owe love to. Write their names down.

_____

_____

_____

_____

Now, think about how you are going to demonstrate to them in a very practical way that you love them with God's love.

DAY FIVE: A MATURE CHRISTIAN SEEKS TO SEE OTHERS AS GOD SEES THEM, AND IS MOVED WITH COMPASSION THE WAY JESUS WAS.

Jesus looked at the city of Jerusalem from the top of the hill and said, *I saw them as sheep without a shepherd wondering around and trying to figure out which direction to go in.* (Matthew 9:36.) Jesus saw them through God's eyes. Even though they were mean, snarled at Him, didn't understand Him, didn't believe Him, and didn't obey Him, He still had supernatural compassion on them. Somebody who is "others" centered begins to see other people as God does. Seeing your friends and your enemies through God's eyes is a sign of maturity. You don't just see them as "Joe" down the street or as "that guy who was picking on me and making fun of me." You see them as precious human beings for whom Jesus died on the cross. Before they were ever picking on you, they were born into this world, and Jesus knew who they were and He wanted to know them. Before they were your life-long friend, they were human beings God saw with His heart of compassion.

Meditate on Matthew 9:36 for five minutes this morning. *When he saw the crowds, he had compassion on them, because they were harassed and helpless, like sheep without a shepherd.*

When you see others the way God does, you will be moved with compassion the way Jesus was you will do whatever you have to do to reach them. Jesus poured out His life. When you love somebody with God's love, the kind of love God has, you'll go to the cross for him, just like Jesus did. You will be very selfless and give yourself away to try to reach them, to minister to them, to care about them.

The problem is that most people today see other people just as if they are looking at animals. In fact, most people in our society value animals more than they value people. We have organizations to protect spotted owls, eagles, and dolphins, but nothing to protect unborn children who are unwanted and aborted. But when Jesus looks at the world He sees people, not only prized possessions. He sees His people who were created in the image of God.

DAY SIX: A MATURE CHRISTIAN DOESN'T CARE WHAT HE WANTS PERSONALLY, BUT WHAT GOD WANTS.

2 Peter 3:9 says, *He is patient with you, not wanting anyone to perish, but everyone to come to repentance.* Think about it for just a moment. God desires for all to come. He wants everybody. He wants them all. A mature Christian is not just thinking about himself. He's thinking about other people as we have been learning all week long. A mature believer cares about other people's souls, about where they are going to spend eternity. God cares about all of them. He wants all of them to come to know Him. And as mature believers we don't just care about what we want, we care about what God wants. God wants people's hearts, God wants their souls, God wants them to be with Him for eternity.

When you start caring about people the way God cares about them, realizing that God wants them for eternity, it will push you to say something. Your heart will well up with compassion because you see people the way He does, like a sheep without a shepherd, and then you realize that He wants them to be with Him forever. Your heart will say, *"I have to say something. I have to pray for them. I have to care about them. I have to find a way to reach out and touch them with the Gospel. With what I say and do, I am going to give myself away. I am going to do whatever I have to do to help them find the knowledge of the truth."*

You reach out through evangelism, not because you feel obligated or because you know you are supposed to do this to be a good Christian, but because your heart is so full of compassion for them that you can't stand the thought of their not going to heaven. This momentum begins to build in your heart and you just can't keep it to yourself anymore.

The epitome of selflessness is caring for people's souls, caring for where they are going to end up eternally the way God does. I want you to think about some people right now and write down their names. Think of people you know are not saved, but you haven't really cared about their souls before. You haven't really cared where they're going to end up for eternity. Write three or four names down and begin to pray for them right now this morning.

_____

_____

_____

_____

_____

_____

_____

_____

Take some time and say, *"God, break my heart for these people. Let me see them the way you do. God, let me start caring about where they are going to spend eternity the way you do."* Ask the Lord for strategies, what to say, what to do to get the message through to them today to live a selfless life so they can come to know Jesus.

Think about it for a moment. How does God look at the people in your math or history class? If you could really see them through God's eyes, what would they look like? What insecurities, frustrations, brokenness do they have in their hearts or lives. What about your teachers? What about the coach you had a hard time with? How does God look at that person? Begin to pray over the people you're going to run into today before you leave your quiet time this morning, and begin to ask God to give you eyes to see each of them the way He does and to treat them accordingly today.

DAY SEVEN: A MATURE CHRISTIAN IS NOT SELF-CENTERED.

We have been talking all week about this whole idea of being selfless, preferring others, caring about their souls, not quarreling and being jealous of them, and owing them love. I hope this week is a pivotal point for you. I want you to take today to review all the Scriptures we have talked about. Write them all down on index cards. Carry them with you today and make a decision from now on to be "others" oriented instead of "self" oriented.

This is not just a nice suggestion, this is an imperative. If you really want to be a mature believer, if you really want to be a tower of strength, if you want to be strategic in the advantage of the Kingdom of God, begin to show signs that you really are growing up as a man or woman of God. You can't keep having everybody cater to your needs and bow to your preferences all the time. You are "others" oriented, giving yourself away because you realize that Jesus cared for you, and in response to His great love you care for other people.

Make this week a pivotal point in your life where you have changed direction. Instead of looking out for your needs, look out for other people's needs. Watch God's blessings blow you away as you continue to grow into a mature believer.

ACTION POINTS

What am I going to do in response to what I learned this week?

_____

_____

_____

_____

_____

_____

_____

MATURITY = GIVING YOURSELF AWAY TO REACH THE WORLD

DAY ONE: WE NEED TO LEARN TO PREFER OTHERS, GIVE OURSELVES AWAY, AND BE SELFLESS.

We talked last week about selflessness being a real sign of maturity. When we are young our whole life revolves around "me," "mine," and "my." We need to learn to prefer others and give ourselves away and be selfless. Well, we are going to notch it up one more level this last week of this devotional.

God is looking for people who will show the ultimate sign of maturity by going overseas and giving themselves away. He wants people who will step out of their own culture to give the Gospel away. No longer do you consider just your own preferences, but you are giving away your time, your whole summer to go on a mission trip. Give up your bed and sleep on a harder bed. Give up your room and sleep in someone else's room. Give up your food preferences and eat the food of another culture. Give yourself away, give your money away, give up your comfort, all so other people can hear the Gospel.

You might not seem to be benefiting from giving yourself away, but other people will get eternal salvation. The fact is, God will bless you, and ultimately you will benefit. One time when Jesus was talking about this the disciples said, But Lord, we have given up our families and our homes and everything. (Mark 10:28-30) *Peter said to him, "We have left everything to follow you!" "I tell you the truth," Jesus replied, "no one who has left home or brothers or sisters or mother or father or children or fields for me and the gospel will fail to receive a hundred times as much in this present age (homes, brothers, sisters, mothers, children and fields—and with them, persecutions) and in the age to come, eternal life."*

Jesus is saying, *"Listen, I'm the one giving the most here."* When you start giving up your home, your family, your comfort you are not going to get anything but blessed. God gets so excited when He sees you giving your life away selflessly that He blesses you back with family, homes, material things, spiritual things, and more. He's looking for people to do what seems like the illogical thing—to give up everything—because those are the people He knows He can trust with everything. When you do that, He will totally bless you and blow you away.

I want you to seriously consider now giving up all the things that you think are important for this summer and go on a mission trip. Think of all the things that seem so convenient to you and all the fun stuff you do in the summer. Give that up to give your life away so other people can know Jesus. And watch to see how God is going to blow you away with blessings as a result.

Take a few minutes to memorize Mark 10:28-30.

DAY TWO: THIS IS YOUR SUMMER TO GO ON A MISSIONS TRIP.

Matthew 16:25: *For whoever wants to save his life will lose it, but whoever loses his life for me will find it.* Spend the next five minutes meditating on this verse.

This is exactly the opposite of what makes sense to the world. The world says, *"Hang onto what is yours. Get as much as you can. Keep yourself in the center of your own life. Try to save your own life."* But God says don't hog things to yourself that you think will make your life happy thinking me, me, me, me, me. Get all you can, can all you get, and sit on your can. Jesus said to do just the opposite. *If you try to save your life. . . .* if you try to do all the things that make up a great life, do all the things the world says will make you happy. In other words, you might have all the stuff, but you'll have an emptiness inside that you can't describe. You will have an empty life, and you will wonder why. You will have everything the world says will make you happy, but you won't have happiness. Jesus says, *if you lose your life for My sake. . . .* That is, if you give everything away, if you're selfless, if you give Me your whole life, your time, your finances, your summer vacations, your energy, if you lose everything for Me, if you become selfless—then you gain real life.

I have never seen this more clearly demonstrated than in young people going on mission trips. They give up what the world says are fun things or popular things that everybody craves to do in the summer. They give up all that and go on a mission trip. People think they are weird, strange. Then these young people come back and talk to their friends and say, *"What did you do this summer?"* Their friends say, *"Ahh, I don't know. Just hung out, just had a job. I can't even remember what I did."* But when they ask that young person who went on a mission trip, *"what did you do?"* he responds, *"Oh, man! I went to this village and people got changed and people got healed and my life was changed and God spoke to me!"* He comes back with real riches you can see in his eyes. You can see it in his heart. Something changed in his life. So the person who thought he was going to have a fun summer, who was trying to save his summer, save his own life, lost it all. He can't even remember what he did. But the young person who gave his life away got real riches.

This summer needs to be your summer. It needs to be the time when you quit hearing about it, quit listening to other people talk about it, quit just feeling convicted about it but not doing anything about it. This is your summer to go. Ask the Lord right now where He wants you to go this summer. Begin to pray about what organization you should go with if your church doesn't already have a youth trip they're taking to another country. Somehow, some way, you need to find a way to go. Sign up on a Teen Mania trip. Do something, just don't stay at home. Give yourself away and show that there's some maturity in you that's driving you to give your life away. And watch out to see how God is going to bless you because of it.

DAY THREE: FEELING SORRY FOR PEOPLE DOESN'T GET THE GOSPEL TO THEM IN ORDER TO THEM TO SAVE THEM.

The Bible says that Jesus was *moved with compassion.* (Matthew 14:14), *And Jesus went forth, and saw a great multitude, and was moved with compassion toward them, and he healed their sick.* As Jesus saw people the way God saw them, He was moved. He couldn't just sit there and look at them and think, *"Oh, those poor people."* It's amazing how many times we have seen video clips or heard stories about people from all over the world who are hurting and desperate for Christ. Not only are they not saved, but they don't even have any way to get saved. There are people all around the world with no Bibles, preachers, pastors, evangelists, missionaries, Christian television or radio programs, Christian bands—nothing.

We hear about them, but virtually we have no compassion in our hearts for them. We think to ourselves, *"Oh, those poor people. It's just too bad."* No, it's not just too bad, it's a tragedy. We hear about them so much we have become callused to their plight, and we think that somebody else will reach them. But that is exactly the problem. Nobody else is reaching them. At least, not very many people are reaching them. We hear stories that should move us to compassion, but we are so self-centered we are not moved at all. We just feel sorry for them. Feeling sorry for them won't save them. Feeling sorry for them won't get the Gospel to them. Feeling sorry for them is not being selfless, it's just a way to justify our selfishness. Our hearts get a little bit sad and maybe we even feel like we will pray for them, but if we are not doing anything to help them with their plight, we are being selfish.

When you think about the needs of the people of the world, going to reach them should just be the natural response. When you're moved with compassion, you should be compelled to do something about it the way Jesus did. Jesus didn't say, *"Oh, those poor people."* He said, *"I've got to go to the cross for those people."* That needs to be our response. It is the natural response of a mature believer. We shouldn't have to be convinced that we really need to go. When we see the people, hear the stories, and see videos, our hearts should be overwhelmed with a compulsion to do something to help reach them. I'm not trying to be "Joe" spiritual, I'm just trying to be a normal Christian who can sense the compassion of God for real people.

Some people think that you have to be an awesome Christian, or mega-spiritual, in order to go on a mission trip. Maybe you don't feel that spiritual so you think you shouldn't go. Going on a mission trip should be normal to people who care about loving God. When you care about the people God loves, you want to do something to reach them.

Write down the names of some countries you might be interested in going to this summer.

_____

_____

_____

_____

_____

_____

It's time to start making some plans to do something this summer with your life to change the world. Start doing research and find a way to get with your church or with some other organization like Teen Mania to get to one of the nations God has put on your heart. It's time to be moved—out of your comfort zone, out of your home town. It's time to be moved with compassion to the harvest field of reaching the world.

DAY FOUR: IF YOU'RE GOING TO MAKE YOUR MARK IN THE WORLD, YOU'RE GOING TO HAVE TO BE SELFLESS.

Luke 10:1-4: *After this the Lord appointed seventy-two others and sent them two by two ahead of him to every town and place where he was about to go. He told them, "The harvest is plentiful, but the workers are few. Ask the Lord of the harvest, therefore, to send out workers into his harvest field. Go! I am sending you out like lambs among wolves. Do not take a purse or bag or sandals; and do not greet anyone on the road."*

This is the passage where Jesus was sending His disciples on a short-term missions trip. They weren't moving out to the mission field for their whole life, they were just going on a short trip. He was sending them out, and He knew they were coming back in just a few weeks.

First of all, Jesus said, *I am sending you out like lambs among the wolves.* You guys are lambs. You are not even sheep yet. You're young, you're lambs. Maybe you feel very young, like you don't know that much about the Lord. You wonder how you could possibly go on a mission trip? You walk by and sometimes you act like you don't have anything between the ears, but that's Okay. Go! Even though you're young as a teenager, God wants you to go because He is going to use you to change the world. So, if you've been wondering if you're too young to go on a mission trip, you should know that Jesus sent people out while they were young.

I want you to see the kind of attitude Jesus sent the disciples out with. He said to go wherever they were sent, stay in the homes, and eat whatever was put before them. He wants you to go with a selfless attitude. Don't go with a self-righteous attitude like you're such a great person because you are going. Jesus says to go with the intentions of giving your life away. Go to serve these people, go to care about them, go to bless them, go to let them know that He really cares about them.

We're talking about being mature believers. A mature believer gives his life away and doesn't ask anything in return. Jesus was trying to show His disciples from the very beginning that if they were going to make their mark on the world, they were going to have to be selfless about it. They were going to have to be willing to give it all away.

It's time for us to get out of our comfort zones and realize that we have to be selfless if we're going to change the world. The mark of real maturity is being much less concerned about yourself and more concerned about others, especially being concerned about whether they turn to salvation. It's time to plan right now to make this summer count.

What have you done about preparing to go on a missions trip this summer?

_____

_____

_____

_____

_____

_____

_____

_____

DAY FIVE: HAVE YOU SENT IN YOUR APPLICATION YET?

Matthew 28:19: *Therefore go and make disciples of all nations, baptizing them in the name of the Father and of the Son and of the Holy Spirit.* This is the Scripture we usually hear when we talk about reaching the world. It is important for us not to get hardened to it. We should never get to the point that we are thinking, *"Yeah, yeah, yeah, the Great Commission, Jesus wants me to go."* If you haven't already, take the time now to memorize Matthew 28:19.

Who do you think Jesus was talking to? He was talking to believers. He is talking to people like you and me, just normal, ordinary people who didn't think they could do very much. He wants you to go and reach the world. In other words, He wants you to place a higher priority on reaching the world than on making your own career, a higher priority on reaching the people Jesus died for than on having a house and car and all the things that are not eternally important. Jesus said that if you seek first the Kingdom, He will add all these things to you. He will bless your face off. He is looking for someone who will put His priority of reaching the world as their own first priority.

The problem with many adults is they have so many obligations it's hard for them to even imagine what it would be like to actually go out and reach the world. They have car payments, house payments, and many other things that they're burdened down with.

These words in Matthew 28:19 are Jesus' parting words. He's trying to leave His disciples with a mandate, an imperative. Now that you guys have grown, now that you have real fire, now that you know what it is like to burn the garbage out of your life and keep going on for God, He's consuming your heart and your life and saying to take that to the world. Take that fire of the presence of the living God that you have burning inside you and don't keep it to yourself. Let people around this globe know that Jesus is real on the inside of you.

This is not the Great Suggestion, it's the Great Commission. Have you sent in your application yet? Have you had your mom and dad sign it yet? If you don't know where to get one, there is a form in the back of this book. Call the 800 number or send the form in today and we will get you an application and you will be on your way.

There are still parts of the world that have never heard of Jesus one time in their life. They don't know that they can go to heaven, that they can have a clean heart, that they can get rid of guilt in their lives. It is going to take somebody who is selfless like you. If you have been through all these weeks finishing up this devotional book and you have applied these things in your life, there is no way you can still be selfish. Now that you have demonstrated that you really do love God and you really do want to go after Him with all your heart, the natural response should be, *"Now, how can I help other people find the same thing?"*

If you haven't done it yet, fill out the application, or call us at 1-800-299-TEEN and we will get you one. Make your life count now. Don't let another day go by wondering what you are going to do this summer. God has big plans for you and it has to do with changing the world. He has been waiting all this time to get you into this position in your heart so you can make a difference. Now go for it.

DAY SIX: A MATURE CHRISTIAN REALIZES THAT THE GREAT COMMISSION IS SPEAKING TO HIM.

Jeremiah 1:5-7: *Before I formed you in the womb I knew you, before you were born I set you apart; I appointed you as a prophet to the nations. "Ah, Sovereign LORD,". I said, "I do not know how to speak; I am only a child." But the LORD said to me, "Do not say, 'I am only a child.' You must go to everyone I send you to and say whatever I command you."*

Watch what the Lord is saying here to Jeremiah. He is saying, *before you were ever born, I had My finger on you because I wanted you to change the world.* The Lord would say the same thing to you. You see, before you were ever a teenager, years ago before you were even born, God had His hand on you. He wanted you to do something great. Maybe you feel like you are just an ordinary person. You feel like He couldn't use you. He said to Jeremiah, *I appointed you a prophet to the nations.* Even though you may feel like an ordinary person, God has had His hand on you for a long time. He's been wanting to use you to make this world a different place.

He said, *I have sent you as a prophet to the nations.* A prophet is somebody who speaks the words of God. Maybe you don't feel like Billy Graham or Oral Roberts, maybe you just feel like a normal person—that's Ok. God says, *"I want you to speak My words to another nation."* There's always a part of us that says, *"But Lord, I am just a child, or I am just a teenager, I can't really do anything, I don't feel very strong in the Lord."* But that doesn't matter. God wants to use you to change the world. He is looking for people who have a real fire down in their heart, a fire that is raging out of control. He's looking for people with a passionate love for Him. Now stand up, be selfless and go give your life and your summer away. Pour yourself out for others and let them know the Gospel is real, alive, and true. It's time to stand up and realize that God has people only you can reach. There's part of the world that will never be reached unless you go. Maybe you'll go on a short-term trip. Maybe you'll go long term for the rest of your life. But at least begin now and just go.

As you mature as a believer, you will see that you're not just a worthless, aimless blob floating through space. You'll realize that God really has had His hand on your life even before you were born, and He really does have a purpose for you here. You're not here just to hang out and go to church the rest of your life but to continue to grow strong, with a passionate love for Him. Then you're here to go and let others know that He is alive, that He is real. God wants to consume their hearts the same way He has consumed yours. A mature believer doesn't just put that command in the hands of somebody else hoping that somebody else will reach them. He realizes that God is speaking to him. He can't just hope somebody else goes and hope somebody else sends. He knows he is going to be part of the answer. He is going to go himself.

I want to see you this summer on a mission trip. I want to see you stand up and be a mature believer who answers the call on your life, even if you just go one time. Once you get a glimpse of the world and see it the way God sees it, you'll never forget it.

DAY SEVEN: MATURITY IS GIVING YOURSELF AWAY TO REACH THE WORLD.

Here we are, you made it. After thirteen weeks, one quarter of the year has gone by and I hope and pray that you have grown as a man or woman in the things of God like never before. I hope that you have grown as a WorldChanger. I pray that you have matured. I am confident that if you have done what we talked about, then you have grown. After writing your action points for this week, go back and make sure you check the action points at the end of each week, at the end of each chapter. Make sure that you're really acting on them. Don't go back to chapter three and find that it's just a vague memory. Make sure there are action points you've been writing down all along, things you're sticking to that you can go back and see week by week milestones of how you've transformed over these last thirteen weeks. How have your attitudes changed? Has the interaction between you and the Lord gotten better? How have things between you and other people changed?

Now, make a final action point on the sheet at the end of this book: What you are going to hang onto and continue to do differently? Take that page out and put it in your Bible to show what you have learned. This will show what you have applied to your life. This is what you're going to continue to do.

Continue growing strong in the Lord, being a mature believer, and making your life count to change this world. Keep feeding your fire. Let it rage out of control and let the world know Who is alive inside of you. Let them wonder at the glimpse of the Eternal God as they see Him through your eyes and your actions. Let your Christianity be something that shines bright. Let your life be the answer to people's prayers for this generation to be changed, for this generation to make a difference. Let your heart continue to be consumed with the fire of the burning presence of God, with a fervor and a fury to find more of Him than you ever dreamed possible. Keep that attitude and you'll be on a firm foundation for an incredible life with God for the rest of your life.

ACTION POINTS

What am I going to do in response to what I learned this week?

_____

_____

_____

_____

SUMMARY OF ACTION POINTS

An overview of what you will do in response to what you learned from this devotional.

_____

_____

_____

_____

_____

_____

_____

_____

_____

_____

_____

_____

Teen Thoughts About Missions

Missions has given me a real sense of purpose and fulfillment.
Greg-Acapulco

I have a clear vision of God's love for all people, and I realize
that I still share God's love with the world,
even if I am not a preacher.
Heather-Albania

Missions has helped me realize the importance
of focusing completely on God.
Angela-Albania

Missions has given me an opportunity to minister Christ's
love to the people of the world.
Jenn-Atlanta

Missions has provided an outlet of ministry for my passion for God.
Jon-Botswana

Teen Mania has given me a call to the mission field
and a relationship to back it up.
Amanda-Botswana

Teen Mania has helped me make my entire life
a ministry wherever I am.
Dawn-Ecuador

If you're not living for God, you're not really living.
Michael-Hong Kong

Missions is to walk in love as Jesus did.
Jessica-Jamaica

If you can save all these people in two weeks, and you don't try
at home, your time is wasted.
Joanna-Mexico

I learned to really trust in Him and let Him be my strength.
Sarah-Panama

Teenagers can change the world.
Alley-Peru

*God has become more real in my life and
my faith in Him is tangible.*
Brenda-Peru

*Missions helped me see the fruit of having a consistent quiet
time. I found myself taking my free time to get alone with God.*
Bryon-Peru

I have learned perseverance and not to quit when things get tough.
Melissa-Thailand

I learned servanthood, obedience and patience.
Christina-Venezuela

*Missions is having every ounce of pride poured out of you until
you're left standing humble before God.*
Catherine-Albania

Missions is giving your heart to the people.
Missy-Albania

Missions is a lot of hard work, fun, and hearing God's voice.
Susie-Botswana

*Missions is reaching out with the power of God's love to people
separated from His love.*
Mike-Botswana

Missions is LOVE—It's all about love.
Jessie-China

Missions is crossing cultural barriers to share God's love.
Melissa-China

Missions is being a mouthpiece of God.
Kim-Ecuador

*Missions is a willingness to get out of your comfort zone. Giving
up what is comfortable for you for the sake of others.*
The Team-El Salvador

Missions is having fun for God.
Becky-Ghana

Missions is learning how to share from your heart.
Cody-Hong Kong

Missions is giving hope to the hopeless.
Couch Potatoes-India

Missions is setting captives free.
Brandi-India

Missions is focus.
Tim-Kazakhstan

Missions is dedication.
Nathan-Mexico

Missions is servanthood.
Ellyn-Mexico

Missions is "I lay ME down."
Ginger-Panama

Missions is going where God has called you and telling people
about Jesus with all your heart.
Bridget-Panama

Missions is doing whatever it takes to tell people about Jesus
and what He did.
Amy-Peru

Missions is going out in the middle of nowhere,
learning the culture, and telling them God loves them.
Lisa-Russia

Missions is taking a step of faith and letting God do the rest.
Gordon-Russia

Missions is being willing to stretch yourself in order
to spread the gospel.
Christina-Thailand

Missions is friends that make a difference.
Kristine-Venezuela

Missions is hard work—The most important work.
Tom-Venezuela

Missions is putting down my wants so that God's will can be done.
Joshua-Vietnam

Missions has given me the commitment to dedicate my heart
and life to God's will.
Ryan-Acapulco

Missions has given me new insight as to our individual
worth to the kingdom.
Greg-Acapulco

Missions has given me compassion.
Tanika-Atlanta

Missions has given me friendships.
Beth-Bolivia

Missions has given me confidence.
Portia-Ecuador

Missions has given me friendships that will last forever.
Shannon-Ecuador

Missions has given me boldness.
Erin-Ecuador

Missions has given me zeal for quiet times.
Sarah-El Salvador

Missions has given me a different look on life.
Clayton-Hong Kong

Missions has given me the realization of the power of prayer.
Dave-India

Missions has given me willingness to work harder.
Jenny-Mexico

Missions has given me a vision for the world.
Jason-Peru

Missions has given me a knowing of how to pray effectively.
Vicki-Russia

Missions has given me passion for God at home.
Bonnie-Venezuela

A family that prays together ends up all over the world!
Carol

Teen Mania has changed my view of what I believed Christianity was.
David-India '94

*Over the past three years, Teen Mania has given me the opportunity
to get a taste of what living life on the edge is all about. Not only has
God started to bring me to an understanding of my calling, but I
have the chance to experience it first hand. . . and the impact.*
Gabe

*On the night of the commissioning service, the Lord told Daniel
that he would lead someone to the Lord using sign language. He
wrote this in his journal, but didn't tell anyone. On our last day
of ministry, we performed the drama for a very small group in an
out of the way village. After wards, while explaining the drama to
individuals, it became apparent that one young girl was deaf and
couldn't understand what we were telling her. As we asked
Daniel to see if he could, he remembered his journal entry. He
proceeded to explain the drama and lead the girl to the Lord
using sign language as the entire team looked on. It was, by far
one of the high points of our time in Acapulco.*
Greg-Acapulco

*As members of Mr. T and the A-Team ministered to the children
after a drama, they had the opportunity to pray for a young boy
who was partially deaf. As a result of their prayers, he is now
whole and able to hear the voice of God.*
Albania

While the R.O.T.C. FREAKS performed the drama at Peidmount Park, a man who had never heard about Jesus stopped to watch. He received Christ as His Savior that day and was overjoyed that he finally got his chance!
Atlanta, GA

The potential of this generation can change the future of their world.
Rich-Botswana

After our last drama in a little village called Shashemooke, an 87-year-old man asked my MIG to pray over him because he was blind. We laid hands on him and prayed, but he wasn't immediately healed. He said he believed God would still heal him, even after we left. I felt in my spirit that God wasn't done yet, so I asked him if he would take a step of faith and get up and walk without a guide. He stood up and started walking toward some houses. I stood about four feet away from him, praying in the Spirit. All of a sudden, he turned and walked towards me. I will never forget the radiant expression of joy on his face! He was yelling excitedly, saying that at first all he could see was snow, and then it became houses. He was healed. Praise God!
Alece—Botswana

My team taught me that with God all things are possible and not to underestimate the power of a teenager.
Angelique—Ecuador

It's amazing how much God can do in someone's life in just one summer.
David-India '94